Mass Communication and Conflict Resolution

W. Phillips Davison

Mass Communication and Conflict Resolution

The Role of the Information Media in the Advancement of International Understanding

PRAEGER SPECIAL STUDIES IN INTERNATIONAL POLITICS AND GOVERNMENT

Praeger Publishers   New York   Washington   London

Library of Congress Cataloging in Publication Data

Davison, Walter Phillips, 1918-
    Mass communication and conflict resolution.

    (Praeger special studies in international politics
and government)
    Bibliography: p. 135
    1. International relations.   2. Mass media.
I. Title.
JX1395.D38   327'.01'41   73-19442

PRAEGER PUBLISHERS
111 Fourth Avenue, New York, N.Y. 10003, U.S.A.
5, Cromwell Place, London SW7 2JL, England

Published in the United States of America in 1974
by Praeger Publishers, Inc.

Printed in the United States of America

ACKNOWLEDGMENTS

Many individuals and organizations have been of assistance in this undertaking. Particular thanks are due to Earl Osborn of the Institute for World Order (formerly the Institute for International Order), who inspired the study as a whole, and to Louis G. Cowan of the Graduate School of Journalism at Columbia University, who helped to determine its basic directions. Moral support and aid of a more concrete nature from three deans of the Graduate School of Journalism must also be acknowledged: Edward W. Barrett, former Dean; Elie Abel, current Dean; and Frederick T. C. Yu, former Associate Dean and an expert in international communication research. A grant from the National Endowment for the Humanities enabled me to revise and extend certain portions of the manuscript.

Major substantive contributions to this inquiry were made by Yonah Alexander, Martin Gershen, Konrad Kellen, and Eugene Lichtenstein, all of whom conducted original research and wrote extensive memoranda on various aspects of the subject under study. Thanks are also due to Donald R. Shanor and Erik N. Valters, who read and commented on portions of the manuscript.

Needless to say, none of the individuals or institutions that assisted in the preparation of this book can be held accountable for its imperfections, content, or findings, which remain my sole responsibility.

CONTENTS

Mass Communication and Conflict Resolution

AN IMMODEST ATTEMPT
TO SOLVE AN OLD PROBLEM

Several years ago, as the result of a grant from the Institute for International Order (now the Institute for World Order) to the Graduate School of Journalism of Columbia University, the writer and a number of colleagues were given an opportunity to explore the role of mass communication in the advancement of world peace. Understandably, we seized the opportunity, feeling that those concerned with communication research and teaching communication skills had an obligation to study how this research and these skills might be put to work in pursuit of one of mankind's most cherished but elusive goals.

But the subject is a difficult one. Communication, as any student of the field is aware, is involved in all forms of social behavior; communication research draws from all the social sciences and from several other disciplines and crafts. Furthermore, any communication must be about something; one cannot escape ultimately dealing with content, and this presupposes knowledge of the phenomena with which communication deals.

Peace is if anything an even more difficult concept, and the study of peace involves all branches of knowledge. The new breed of peace researchers, now rapidly multiplying, includes social scientists of all stripes, lawyers, philosophers, natural scientists, and many others. Almost no aspect of human experience is exempt from their inquiries. When one bundles together the concept of communication and the concept of peace, the resulting research package represents a major challenge.

As if to complicate the problem still more, we hoped to emerge with some suggestions for action. The major focus was not to be on gathering new data but on putting to work what was known or what could be learned fairly quickly in order to suggest steps that might be considered by the mass media, peace organizations, universities, the United Nations, the U.S. government, and any other organizations that might be in a position to use communications in the advancement of international understanding.

This may be a reasonable goal for an applied research project, but it is clearly an ambitious one. Countless persons of good will and intelligence have worked untiringly in the pursuit of peace, and many of them have also been skilled in the communication arts. Any easily discoverable suggestions of a practical nature would already have been formulated, and possibly tried and adopted or rejected. The ground has been well picked over. On several occasions we have had the experience of combing through masses of technical literature only to emerge with a generalization considerably better known than the literature itself. To cite one such experience, the writer spent several days reading materials on communication in conflict resolution, accumulating many pages of notes. When translated from the jargon that many of us in this trade use, these notes said, in effect: "A soft answer turneth away wrath."

And even if we could come up with a few suggestions or shed a little new light on old truths, would this justify the time and effort involved? Communication has proved to be a rather weak instrument. We know that it can rarely affect deep-seated attitudes and values. An information campaign cannot force one nation to stop coveting the territory of another, or eliminate the causes of long-standing enmity; usually it cannot even change many votes in a national election. Scholars have found it extremely difficult to demonstrate that violence on TV stimulates greater violence in children. They now appear to have demonstrated that there is a fairly weak relationship, but it has been a long, hard task. (Bogart, 1972-73.) If the relationship between televised violence and behavior is so tenuous, what right have we to expect that communication can make men more peaceful or can help them resolve their conflicts?

The common-sense answer to this objection is that, when a goal is sufficiently important, anything is worth trying, even if the chances of success are low. Perhaps not very much can be accomplished through communication to bring about a more peaceful world, but if anything at all can be done then we should seek the means of doing it. Members of the U.S. Office of War Information used this argument in justifying their work during World War II, when it was criticized by those who felt it was at best a waste of time and at worst a diversion of national resources. If they could shorten the war by a single day through propaganda, these people said, the effort that went into their news releases, leaflets, radio broadcasts, and information libraries would be worthwhile.

This argument is strengthened somewhat by the relatively low cost of communication. Even color television is a far less expensive instrument of policy than a military or economic instrument. Radio and the print media are still more economical. Low cost means wider accessibility. Not only national governments but private groups of fairly modest means might make better use of mass communication if they knew more about how to employ it. A search for ways to make more constructive use of this low-cost instrument therefore seems worthwhile.

Such a search appears to be particularly appropriate at the present time, when social and political conditions throughout the world are in a state of rapid flux. Technological developments affecting both war-making and communication have presented us with a situation mankind has never before encountered. A historian, noting that much of the existing international law governing war had been overtaken by events and was no longer applicable, has concluded, "The preservation of peace must be assured through means and in dimensions that we have hitherto been unable to visualize." (Schieder, 1968, pp. 894-95.) Thus there are at least some grounds for hoping that the relative ineffectiveness of mass communication in helping to resolve past conflicts does not mean that it cannot be a valuable instrument under the new conditions prevailing today and tomorrow.

Despite these and other reasons why research on the role of mass communication in the advancement of international understanding would seem worthwhile, social scientists have devoted surprisingly little effort to this avenue of inquiry. A bibliography, covering articles published during the 1944-64 period in 48 journals that deal in some way with the mass media, includes only two items with the word "peace" in their titles. (Danielson and Wilhoit, Jr., 1967.) One is Bernard Cohen's "Political Communication on the Japanese Peace Settlement," published in the Public Opinion Quarterly in 1956 (vol. 20, no. 1). The other is J. A. Fosdick's "Photography in War and Peace" (Journalism Quarterly 24, no. 2). Searches under other likely headings—such as "conflict," "war," and "understanding"—yielded similarly meager results.

Nor do the journals devoted to problems of war and peace prove a very much richer source. Such publications as the Journal of Conflict Resolution, the Journal of Peace Research, and War/Peace Report have published few articles that deal directly with the potential role of the mass media as a force for or against peace. However, the articles that have been published on this subject include a number of valuable ones, and a number of others are highly suggestive even if not directly applicable to the problem at hand.

As this relative lack of attention to communication would suggest, the news media have been of little interest to peace researchers.

According to a mail survey published by the International Peace Research Institute, Oslo, in 1965, only 17 out of 65 institutions specializing in work on conflict resolution reported that they were doing or had done research in the field of news communication (another 26 did not answer this question at all). Most of those displaying some interest in the mass media appeared to be using the media as information sources on topics other than the role of the news itself. (Ostgaard, 1965, p. 39.) A brief summary of peacekeeping proposals prepared for the Friends Peace Committee in 1969 contained only one reference to mass communications; this was that an alliance of disarmed nations might be supported by propaganda, among other instruments. (Walker, 1969.) Between January 1969 and May 1970 the U.S. Arms Control and Disarmament Agency received 158 requests for the support of Ph.D. dissertations with some relationship to research on arms control or conflict resolution. Of these, only six showed a major concern with communication, and none of the six was given support. (The writer has not read the proposals submitted and merely judged their subject matter from their titles. It may be that some additional proposals were concerned with communication even though their titles did not make this clear.)

The historical literature contains some fascinating material on the role of the press in international conflict, but this testimony provides few suggestions about the way the press could help reduce conflict in the present era. There is the story of the Ems telegram: Prussian Chancellor Bismarck, seeking to provoke France to declare war, edited a telegram from his king in such a way that it would be highly insulting to the French emperor. Then he leaked the text to the Paris press—and France declared war. The activity of some sectors of the U.S. press in facilitating war between the United States and Spain in 1898 is familiar to historians. Atrocity propaganda, willingly carried by the mass media of the contending nations during World War I, has been well documented. The list of examples could be extended to book length.

But one can scarcely regard the insights obtained from such historical accounts as new or as necessarily applicable under current conditions. With war so much more terrible than it was in the days of Bismarck, a conflict can no longer be incited by publicizing an insult to a monarch or head of state. That the press should refrain from fanning war hysteria by circulating false or distorted reports is well recognized; while there are still occasional breaches of journalistic ethics in this regard, it is not because the dangers of journalistic irresponsibility are unknown. Similarly, unrestrained atrocity propaganda became rare following World War I, at least in countries with a free press. Atrocities still occurred, and were reported, but much more soberly and with more careful attention to facts and verification.

The "dos" and "don'ts" for the press that can be deduced from the historical record appear obvious, and journalists by and large have taken them into account. The media are now faced with a series of difficult questions that have no clear answers. In view of the responsibility of the press for informing the public, when is it justified in withholding information that might inflame relations between states? How much checking should a journalist do before using a politician's statement that might prove mischievous? (If he devotes too much time to verification, his competitor may reach the public first with an even more one-sided story.) How much should the mass media try to simplify complex problems in order to make them comprehensible to a broad public? These and other questions currently faced by journalists have a bearing on war and peace, but the historical record provides no easy answers. Nor does past experience help us very much in determining how new communication technologies might serve to advance international understanding.

Although there is thus little literature that is directly addressed to the problem of how the mass media can be used in nonviolent conflict resolution, the amount of writing that is in some way relevant to the problem is enormous and no single study could hope to encompass all of it.

The range of subject matter involved is suggested by Quincy Wright, who observes that many students who do not believe war is inevitable see governments as reaching decisions in given situations "through processes of information gathering, analysis, evaluation, and consultation—all influenced by the decision-makers' images, assumptions, and prejudices." He also observes that the maintenance of peace depends "on a correct image of the world as a whole, and on the guidance of political decisions . . . by knowledge of the probable reaction of each of the systems of action able to precipitate hostilities." (Wright, 1968, pp. 465-66.) While Wright does not specifically name the mass media in his analysis, one immediately suspects that they may be highly relevant to decisions affecting war and peace through their ability to inform, describe, support or combat prejudices, and link together various political systems. Indeed there is scarcely any observation about war and peace that cannot be related to aspects of communication.

Either of two approaches would therefore be possible. One approach would be to explore cases of violent conflict and cases of peaceful solutions, noting the role of mass communication in each and, hopefully, arriving at a number of generalizations about ways the mass media could promote peace. Alternatively, one could inventory what is known about the processes and effects of communication and then ask how the media might contribute to the resolution of international conflict in varying types of situations.

5

We finally decided to adopt the second approach, both because the first would have involved collecting and analyzing vast quantities of data and because we were already relatively familiar with the literature on communication. This approach led directly to three questions:

What are the capabilities of the mass media when it comes to influencing human behavior? How, in theory at least, could these capabilities facilitate the prevention and resolution of conflict? What organizations might be in a position to make use of mass communication to these ends?

For the purpose of our inquiry we did not adopt a formal definition of "peace" but rather tried to look at the war-peace continuum, with general war at one end and a stable situation at the other. A stable situation was defined as one that satisfied two conditions: (1) absence of conflict between two or more parties and (2) satisfaction of those parties with their relationship. Obviously, there are many instances in which little or no conflict is discernible but a stable situation cannot be said to obtain. Race relations in some areas of the American South prior to the civil rights movement provide one example; the relationship between a poor and dissatisfied state that is formally at peace with a rich neighbor is another.

Any move along the continuum away from general war and toward a stable situation was regarded as a worthwhile goal in our research. Few if any examples of completely stable situations can be found in the world today. Some relationships, however, come close to that end of the continuum: for example, the relationships among members of the European Common Market. We have thus considered peace more a direction than a condition. We believe that conflict among states will continue, but that ways to resolve this conflict without violence can be found.

A Brief Summary

The reasoning in this analysis is as follows: Decisions affecting war and peace are made by governments, and the mass media play a significant if limited role in shaping these decisions. They exercise this influence through their ability to cut through bureaucracy and reach governmental leaders directly with information about the world situation; through their capacity to affect official priorities; and through their power to help mobilize public opinion, which decision-makers must take into account.

In theory, at least, the media could increase the quantity and quality of the information that leaders and publics in each nation have about other nations; they could provide early warning of dangerous situations and could point out opportunities for strengthening international understanding; they could encourage the use of negotiation, mediation, and other mechanisms for conflict resolution, and facilitate the work of negotiators and mediators; they could help to bring about states of mind in which peaceful solutions would be more readily sought and accepted; and they could play a part in the mobilization and encouragement of individuals and organizations seeking to strengthen international understanding.

The international press sometimes does perform these functions, but its capacity to do more is limited by the paucity of news sources from which it can obtain precisely those types of information that are of greatest importance in connection with conflict resolution: that is, information that will provide early warning of dangerous situations, assist in getting negotiations started, and so on. The performance of the press is also lowered somewhat by the commonly accepted definition of news, by the use of slogans and stereotypes, and by the parochialism of most mass media. But responsibility for these shortcomings cannot be assigned to the press alone; it must be shared by the public.

Three categories of groups in the private sector can help the mass media become a more effective instrument in the advancement of international understanding. These include groups devoted to the pursuit of peace, academic area research institutes, and organizations engaging in communication research. The first two can make more accessible to the press the kinds of information that it now has difficulty in obtaining; communication researchers can experiment with new modes for the presentation of news and information that are likely to be of assistance in conflict resolution—for example, the televising of political games and the adaptation to public forums of techniques found useful in promoting agreement among members of small groups.

Governments can assist the mass media by making available more of the information that is now classified or otherwise withheld from the press, and by using their resources to promote more two-way public communication among nations.

The United Nations, especially through the secretary-general and the Office of Public Information, could do more to focus the attention of policy-makers in all countries on problems urgently in need of solution and on possibilities for conflict resolution. The U.N. could also play a part in improving the quality of international reporting and devising new modes of effective two-way communication among nations.

Can the mass media help to bring peace to such a severely troubled area as the Middle East? Not alone, certainly, but properly used they might well hasten a solution that would be acceptable to all parties concerned.

2

THE POWER
OF THE MEDIA

Although it is usually impossible to predict with any confidence the exact effect that a particular communication will have on a given individual or group, the kinds of effects that the mass media can achieve have been fairly well established.* These effects can be categorized in various ways, but we will group them under five rubrics. Communications can: (1) raise the information level; (2) focus attention on certain subjects and provide priorities and terminology for thinking about them; (3) affect attitudes, although only under certain conditions; (4) help create a mood or a frame of mind; and (5) enable organizations, including public opinion, to take shape and function.

Perhaps the most important task of the media is to provide people with information about the world around them, especially the world that is beyond the scope of their direct experience and that they cannot observe directly. Most people in industrialized societies gain

---

*Few direct references to the research literature will be made here because a listing of even the more important studies would run to several hundred items. For summary treatments of the effects of communications, see Joseph T. Klapper, The Effects of Mass Communication (Glencoe, Ill.: Free Press, 1960); Otto N. Larsen, "Social Effects of Mass Communication," in Robert E. L. Faris, ed., Handbook of Modern Sociology (Chicago: Rand McNally, 1964); W. Phillips Davison, International Political Communication (New York: Praeger Publishers, 1965); Walter Weiss, "Effects of the Mass Media of Communication," in Gardner Lindzey and Elliot Aronson, eds., Handbook of Social Psychology, Vol. 5, (2nd ed.; Reading, Mass.: Addison-Wesley, 1968), pp. 77ff.

the bulk of their knowledge about national and international affairs from television, newspapers, and magazines. The average American learns most of what he knows about communism from the mass media, and citizens of communist countries are heavily dependent on the press for information about capitalism. In general, the more distant a particular subject is from the direct experience of the individual, the more he must rely on journalists to describe and interpret it for him. And since international affairs are very distant from the personal experience of most people throughout the world, the importance of the mass media in informing them about this sphere is particularly great.

Information often leads to action. A person who learns that a product he wants is on sale is likely to go and buy it. News that a storm is approaching will lead him to take precautions against rain and wind damage. Advice on how to improve health or appearance, farming techniques or reading speed, will often be acted upon. A political report may trigger a politically relevant action, causing a person to vote in a certain way or to write to his congressman.

Communications that lead to expectations about future events can sometimes bring about the events predicted. Reports that a bank is likely to fail may induce depositors to withdraw their money—with the result that the bank fails. A self-fulfilling prophecy has been made. If people belonging to a particular minority group are uniformly characterized as stupid, they will be treated as though they were stupid, and their performance is likely to be below average. Individuals who are publicly labeled superior may turn in a superior performance because it is expected of them.

Conversely, information about future events may lead to behavior that ensures that the predicted events do not occur.

Predictions of severe epidemics have often led to mass vaccination or inoculation. Rumors that a given bank is about to fail are ordinarily scotched by banking officials who provide assurances that the bank is in sound condition.

Thus, while information often leads to action, the relationship between the information, the action, and the subsequent events is often complex and the net effect of the information may be impossible to predict.

Another way information influences behavior is by arousing new desires and new perceptions of opportunities or possibilities. Advertising has helped to create new needs, leading to a demand for new products. (Who, a generation ago, ever thought of asking for an anti-perspirant?) Millions of Europeans were drawn to the New World by rosy depictions of the possibility of a new existence. Today the mass media bring a picture of industrialized societies to people in developing countries, leading them to question the inevitability of their traditional way of life as they visualize themselves driving cars, wearing fine clothes, and giving up back-breaking toil in the fields.

As well as providing information, the mass media offer guidelines for thinking about this information. How important is it? How seriously should we take it? In what terms should we think about it? Events reported in the newspaper headlines or featured on evening news broadcasts are likely to be discussed. As Bernard Cohen has put it, the press may not be very successful in telling us what to think but it is highly successful in telling us what to think about. (Cohen, 1960, p. 165; Cohen, 1963, pp. 224-29.) For example, most of the mail received by the U.S. State Department and White House deals with subjects currently, or at least recently, in the headlines.

Just as the mass media indicate how important certain events or subjects are, they also provide a rough scale for ranking the importance of individuals. If a person is important, he will be in the news; if he is in the news, he must be important (Lazarsfeld and Merton, 1948, pp.101-2.) As a result of this circular reasoning, which is common among consumers of the press, the media can confer prestige, often building up a nonentity into a public figure. And even some journalists are deceived by their own skill in creating personalities, accepting the authority of those whom they have almost accidentally projected into the public eye. The circular process thus starts all over again.

When we think or write about a subject the press has brought to our attention, we are likely to use the terminology we have learned from the media. When scholars interviewed refugees who left the Soviet Union after World War II, they found that even those who were strongly opposed to communism used the terminology employed by the Soviet press and radio. To them, the two world wars were the "First Imperialist War" and the "Second Imperialist War," and so on. Similarly, Americans in Germany at the time found anti-Nazi Germans using slogans popularized by Propaganda Minister Joseph Goebbels. Although we may not be conscious of it, nearly all of us have incorporated into our vocabularies and our ways of thinking some of the short-cuts and labels used by the headline writers.

But the mass media do not seem to have a very great effect on well-established attitudes. When people have strong political or religious preferences, even large amounts of information or propaganda are unlikely to shake them. In 1932, 1936, and 1940, most American newspapers backed the Republican presidential candidate, but each time Franklin D. Roosevelt was easily elected. In 1960, John F. Kennedy won electin with the support of only 15 percent of the dailies published in the country.

Numerous experimental studies have led to the same conclusion: When attitudes are strongly held, communications by themselves usually cannot cause the attitudes to be significantly modified. The media are likely to change the direction of a strongly held attitude only when they are able to report some change that makes the attitude inappropriate. Thus, when a government previously regarded as unfriendly is reported to have changed to a much more friendly posture, people tend to adjust their attitudes accordingly, as U.S. public opinion did following the relaxation of relations with China. Similarly, public opinion researchers have found that American attitudes toward integrated schools became much more favorable after integration had been ordered, presumably because the old anti-integration attitudes had been overtaken by events and no longer served a useful purpose for many of those who had held them. But by itself propaganda is not usually powerful enough to change attitudes, especially when it does not enjoy a monopoly of the channels of communication.

On the other hand, communications can often affect weakly held attitudes and can be important in creating new attitudes. In elections where the public is not aroused and where little information about candidates or issues is available, newspaper editorials may be important in swinging the vote one way or another. Similarly, political propaganda has been found to influence attitudes toward national parties much more between elections, when the salience of issues and personalities is relatively low, than it can just before elections, when emotions are running high. And if a person has no opinion and very little information on a given subject, then almost any communication on that subject is likely to be influential in molding his attitude. Thus, the reports of explorers, often biased or incomplete, have been very influential in shaping mass attitudes toward primitive societies or newly discovered parts of the world. People were interested in the new discoveries but had no other sources of information on which to base their attitudes.

Perhaps the most important effect of communications, as far as attitudes are concerned, is to activate and reinforce existing tendencies. If people already fear or distrust a given government, it is relatively easy to use mass communications to fan and increase this fear and distrust. Or, if they are favorably disposed toward a political figure or a commercial product, their favorable predispositions can be increased and often they can be activated to vote for the politician in question or buy the product. Propagandists who advocate appealing to the emotions rather than to reason are in fact referring to the ability of communications to reinforce and activate existing attitudes. Before this can be done, of course, the propagandist must find out exactly what the existing attitudes are, which is why large-scale information or propaganda campaigns are often preceded by audience research.

11

There is a widely shared tendency for people to believe that propaganda influences attitudes and behavior more than it actually does. This leads to what may be called the "third person effect." That is, one group attempts to persuade a second group of something, and a third group then assumes that persuasion is actually taking place—whether this is the case or not—and acts accordingly. This is one reason why leaders of established religions have been so concerned about heretical doctrines. They have assumed that these doctrines were actually finding converts and therefore they have resorted to extreme suppressive measures. Governments often react in a similar manner and through suppression give more currency to dissident propaganda than it would otherwise receive. The third person effect may lead to verbal duels between propagandists, each of whom assumes that the other's words are more influential than they actually are. Since this category of communication effect has not as yet been studied systematically, the extent of its influence in relations among nations is not known, but it may prove to be of considerable significance. One can visualize situations in which one nation's policy toward another may be based, at least in part, on the assumption that the government and people of the second nation are being influenced by propaganda from a third party.

Regardless of the extent to which mass communications can influence the content of individual attitudes, they are often able to affect the mood of individuals or large groups. A steady diet of stories about disasters, corruption, and stupidity can stimulate a mood of anger, pessimism, or despair, while a preponderance of encouraging news can lead to a much more hopeful mood. This principle is well known to troop commanders, who try to maintain a balance of encouraging communications within their units, and to the opposing psychological warfare personnel, who try to ensure that discouraging communications predominate. Again, little systematic work has been done on the role of communications in creating a general mood, but it appears probable that this capability could significantly affect the climate in which proposals affecting war and peace are debated.

A final observation about the effects of the mass media—one that is often overlooked because it is so obvious—is that communication makes it possible for large groups to form and holds them together after they have taken shape. This is as true of formal organizations, such as factories or political parties, as it is of informal groups of like-minded people. A commercial organization usually has to make use of the mass media to recruit workers, sell products, and maintain good relations with various sectors of the public. It may also use the press to keep track of what its competitors and government authorities are doing. Political parties rely even more heavily on the mass media, and a party or candidate without adequate communications has great difficulty in gaining supporters and bringing them to the polls at election time. Even religious organizations are often dependent on mass communication to keep their adherents together—some of the earliest newspapers in Europe were founded by denominations whose memberships were scattered geographically. During World War II, partisan groups in German-occupied Europe were stimulated, and their activities coordinated, by radio broadcasts from London. Without this channel they would have been less effective.

Public opinion, which may be seen as a form of organization, is also dependent on mass communication. Before individual opinions on a given subject can be molded into a mass opinion, people have to learn what others are thinking and saying about the subject in question. They have to learn that many others share—or disagree with—their opinions, and who the opinion leaders are. Their attitudes are reinforced by the media, and by the knowledge that they are not alone in holding them. Where there are no mass media, public opinion forms much more slowly and on fewer subjects, or it may not form at all.

Until relatively recently, for example, mass media have given little attention to the problems presented by a rapidly expanding population. Therefore few people were organized into groups holding strong opinions on this subject. Only opponents of birth control and abortion were conscious of their strength. Rapidly increasing media attention then enabled public opinion in favor of population control to crystallize, and this gained sufficient strength to lead to changes in the law in several parts of the world. The relationship between publicity and public opinion on population control is implicitly recognized in a report on the subject by a panel of the United Nations Association of the United States:

> The press, radio, television, and movies can play an important part in legitimizing the concept of family planning and in developing broad community acceptance of the principles of responsible parenthood. UNESCO should provide technical advice about the use of mass media in family planning programs and design major projects in this area. [United Nations Association—U.S.A., 1969, p. 47.]

There are many such subjects: subjects on which individual opinions exist, some of them very strong, but these individual opinions have not come into the focus of public attention sufficiently for a public opinion to form.

This catalog of the effects of mass communication may look more impressive than it actually is, mainly because these are potential effects that may be realized under some conditions and not under others. The major limiting factor on the effect of communications

13

is the ability of the individual to disregard or discount almost any information to which he is exposed. Or he may not choose to expose himself at all. Students have been amazed at the extent to which massive information or propaganda campaigns can flow over a mass public and leave almost no trace. This usually occurs when most people are not interested; they may see or hear some of the communications but immediately forget them because they have no relevance to personal interests. But if their interest can be aroused, the effects may be substantial.

Furthermore, even when the mass media achieve certain effects, different individuals and groups may be affected very differently. By and large, "hawks" and "doves" read the same newspapers and view the same television programs, but the conclusions they draw vary considerably. This is largely because each person tends to select from the stream of communications to which he is exposed the facts or ideas that are likely to be useful to him in some way. They may support his existing opinions, giving him a sense of reassurance; they may tell him how to do something he wants to do anyway; or they may provide him with information he can use in conversation. If a communication has no utility for a given individual, he is likely to disregard it or forget it rather quickly. Limited exceptions to this generalization do occur: If a political or commercial slogan is repeated often enough it is likely to be retained by many who are exposed to it, but if the slogan is of little interest it will be forgotten shortly after repetition is discontinued. To a certain extent, the mass media manipulate people, but to an even greater extent people manipulate the mass media.

Mass communication can affect behavior powerfully, moderately, or not at all. The effects depend in part on the skill with which communications are composed and the extent to which they are disseminated, but even more on the predispositions of those exposed to them and on the ability or inability of these people to take the actions suggested. A wise politician does not waste his money on election propaganda in districts where he knows the voters are solidly behind his opponent; neither does he spend his time appealing for the votes of those who for one reason or another are disenfranchised. Instead, he usually concentrates on districts where voters are known to be wavering in their loyalties and where persuasion of relatively few will give him a majority. And most of all he devotes his campaign appeals to arousing the enthusiasm of his supporters and ensuring that they go to the polls on election day.

The problem facing those who would make greater use of the mass media in the advancement of international understanding is to identify relevant audiences, to specify actions that people in these audiences might take in order to resolve conflicts peacefully, and then to devise ways of reaching these people with messages that will bring about the desired behavior.

14

3

THE PRIMARY AUDIENCES:
DECISION-MAKERS AND
THOSE WHO INFLUENCE THEM

Even if the media are important in shaping the information, attitudes, and behavior of the public, this would not necessarily mean that they are influential in questions affecting war and peace. Contrary to the concept, popularized in the preamble to the United Nations Educational, Scientific and Cultural Organization (UNESCO) charter, that wars begin in the minds of men and that it is there that the defense of peace must be constructed, war and peace result from decisions made by governments. (Dunn, 1950.) It is therefore important to inquire whether mass communications enter significantly into these decisions.

As far as can be determined, they do enter in at several points: They help to set the agenda for political leaders, as they do for the general public; they provide these leaders with much of the information on which decisions are based; they likewise influence the experts and "elites" who in turn influence the decision-makers; they affect public opinion on specific issues and the public mood in general, thus limiting or expanding the alternatives that political leaders can realistically consider; and they provide the channels through which governments must explain their policies in order to obtain the consent or cooperation of the governed.

The ability of mass communications to help set the priorities of governments and to influence the daily agenda of decision-makers has been noted by Bernard Cohen. When the press gives prominence to an issue, this tends to nudge it somewhat higher on the list of items claiming the attention of foreign policy officials. (Cohen, 1963, p. 229.) He found, indeed, that at the time of his study one of the most influential documents prepared in the U.S. State Department was a daily summary of newspaper headlines that was circulated to high foreign policy officials prior to the department's staff meeting. The influence of the press on priorities is also exercised through the questions that reporters ask, and for which answers must be found. Stories featured by television or the daily press stimulate mail to government agencies and this, too, must be answered. The mass media can divert a top official from matters he considers most important and force him to deal with a controversy he regards as minor; they can also make him face up to important issues he might prefer to ignore. Either way, the influence of the media on priorities is considerable.

This attention-getting capability of the media is occasionally used by subordinate officials to convey messages to their superiors. In some instances, diplomats who have found it impossible to secure action from their governments by commenting through regular diplomatic channels have told their troubles to the press. The resulting stories have often been able to secure the attention of decision-makers in the capital.

MASS COMMUNICATION AS A SOURCE OF INFORMATION

Although decision-makers normally have many channels of information available to them, including reports prepared by government agencies and intelligence networks, most of them rely heavily on normal news channels. Wire service tickers are installed in the offices of high government officials, and in this way they often receive news of important events hours or even days before word about the same events reaches them through official channels. Officials also tend to be heavy consumers of the press, both directly and indirectly. They read and watch as much as they can themselves, and there are few large governmental agencies that do not prepare a press summary of items likely to be of interest to the top decision-makers.

Most American presidents appear to pay close attention to the mass media in one way or another. Former President Lyndon B. Johnson noted that his typical day at the White House began with reading the morning papers at breakfast (Johnson, 1971 p. 493) and Mrs. Johnson confirmed that her husband paid close attention to both newspapers and television broadcasts, in an interview with Howard K. Smith of ABC News on November 15, 1970. President Nixon is reported to rely mainly on a daily news summary that runs to several dozen pages of typewritten copy. This summary includes stories from many newspapers, magazines, and television news shows; fifty copies are circulated within the White House (Buchanan, 1971; Diamond, 1971). On occasion, President Nixon also receives summaries of mass media content from other countries as, for instance, during his trip to China in 1972. (U.S.I.A. World, 1972.)

Even intelligence reports and diplomatic dispatches are heavily dependent on the mass media. Admiral Zacharias, chief of naval intelligence during World War II, used to say that 90 percent of all intelligence is derived from a careful reading of the press. Allan Dulles, long-time director of the Central Intelligence Agency, has confirmed that government intelligence is largely based on newspapers, books, and magazines. (Dulles, 1963.) Diplomats, too, usually make extensive use of the mass media in countries where they are stationed when they write reports for their superiors. This fact led one U.S. foreign service officer to suggest whimsically that the best way to improve diplomatic reporting would be to improve journalism in foreign countries (Donovan, 1963). Another foreign service officer notes that analyses prepared at embassies abroad must now compete as never before with those from journalists and other sources that may reach government officials first (G. Fisher, 1972, p. 4.) Legislators, since fewer special reports are prepared for them, depend even more on the facilities of the press than do executive agencies. At one point during the 1960s, the staff of the Senate Foreign Relations Committee turned for news about Vietnam to a private weekly communication provided to them by Time magazine's Saigon correspondent. More commonly, senators and their staffs rely mainly on public media channels for information about what is going on in the world.

The extent to which government officials rely on commercial news media has led some students of foreign policy to conclude that the quality of governmental decisions is closely related to the quality and quantity of press coverage. Thus, an academic expert on Eastern Europe has observed that because American newspaper and magazine coverage of Eastern Europe is very thin, an intelligent American foreign policy toward Eastern Europe is exceedingly difficult. Students of African and Latin American affairs have made similar observations. (Yu, 1963.)

Most information that reaches high officials is filtered for them by subordinates, and in this process selectivity or outright prejudice may introduce bias. The ability of the mass media to reach decision-makers directly offers a valuable, if limited, means of short-circuiting the bureaucratic network and partially alleviating the isolation of top policy-makers. George Reedy, at one time President Johnson's press secretary, characterized the press as the only force entering the White House from the outside world that has a direct impact on the chief executive and that "cannot be softened by intermediary interpreters or deflected by sympathetic attendants. . . ." (Small, 1970, p. 230.) At the White House and at lower levels of government, it is common for officials to learn about a particular event or idea from an item in the mass media and then to ask subordinates to explore it further. The ability of the press to introduce new ideas into the decision-making

17

process is particularly important since many bureaucrats are reluctant to "rock the boat." Indeed, the bureaucrat who advances a proposal that departs from existing policy may imperil his career by doing so— as one observer has remarked, "it is poor strategy to make suggestions which are not adopted. . . . The safest bet is to be opposed to change." (R. Fisher, 1969, p. 185.)

Journalists are not unmindful of their roles as purveyors of policy-relevant information to officialdom. CBS correspondent Walter Cronkite, in discussing the importance of informed decision-makers, observes that the mass media can provide them with information that "it would take them far too long to get . . . if indeed they ever got— through secret communications." (Cronkite, 1969, p. 18.)

The mass media influence governmental decisions indirectly through elite groups—those groups inside and outside the government that share in the process of policy initiation and formulation although they do not make the final decisions. (Almond, 1960, pp. 139 ff.) Members of elite groups are precisely those who are the heaviest consumers of mass communications about foreign affairs. The higher officials of the bureaucracy, representatives of major lobbies, leading business-men, and prominent educators are all likely to read a newspaper that emphasizes international coverage, to subscribe to magazines that include a great deal of information on events abroad, and to give more attention than the average citizen to "serious" programming on radio and television. A survey made some ten years ago found that nearly half the persons listed in Who's Who in America gave the New York Times as their favorite newspaper, and there is no reason to believe that the situation has changed. (Kraft, 1961.) In the United States, the "elite press" includes the Times, the Washington Post, the Wall Street Journal, the Christian Science Monitor, and a few other papers, as well as various more specialized journals. A similar "elite press" exists in almost every country.

While those who influence governmental decisions do not necessarily espouse opinions expressed by the mass media, they rely even more than do the decision-makers themselves on information provided by the public communication network. The more influential these elites are, the more communications they are likely to pay attention to. In this way, the direct impact of the media on decision-makers is reinforced. Reports about a brewing crisis in foreign trade may not lead directly to a governmental decision, but they may activate those whose interests are affected to demand a decision. Similarly, the scholar who advocates a certain course of foreign policy is likely to base much of his argument on press reports.

THE MEDIA'S ROLE IN SHAPING PUBLIC OPINION

In contrast to the elites, most citizens pay little attention to international affairs. In the United States and other industrialized nations, those who give serious attention to events outside their own country are usually estimated to comprise about 15 percent of the adult population. In developing countries, the "attentive public" is considerably smaller. Nevertheless, the mass public still exercises considerable influence on governmental decisions. If a country's mood is isolationist, a government will be hesitant about making commitments abroad. If the mood is jingoist, the government may find it difficult to conduct a prudent foreign policy.

Franklin D. Roosevelt was restrained from intervening in Europe during the initial stages of World War II by the knowledge that intervention was unlikely to find mass support. But his successors in the 1950s had to beware of appearing to be "soft on communism," since the country's mood had changed. A remark often attributed to Egyptian President Nasser—that he could make peace with Israel in five minutes but then he could not return home—emphasizes the impact of public mood on the policy-maker.

A U. S. foreign service officer recently wrote that in an era of mass communication "the decision maker and the negotiator find their range of alternatives constrained by the mood and viewpoint of their interested publics." They must search for agreements that will be accepted at home as well as abroad. (G. Fisher, 1972, p. 4.)

The mass media not only help to establish a public mood; they also reflect it. A circular process is involved. Nevertheless, even in a circular process each element plays a role and communications that merely register a public mood also serve to augment it.* Journalists who report popular trust or distrust in a government thereby tend to increase or decrease that government's credibility, and consequently affect its freedom of action.

When it comes to mobilizing opinion on specific issues, the mass media may serve as a tool of government or they may exercise a form of pressure on government. That is, political leaders may use the

---

*An editor of Der Spiegel, a German news magazine previously known for its cynical, sarcastic tone, told the writer in 1955 that the magazine adopted this tone because "that's the way people are at the present time." Insofar as such tendencies did exist among Der Spiegel's readership, they must have been heightened by the material to which they were exposed since we know that attitudes are usually reinforced by supporting communications. In addition, the popularity of Der Spiegel probably led other publications to imitate its style.

media to build support for their aims; or the media may make it possible for those who advocate policy changes to rally a body of opinion that the government must take into account. Either way, the media influence decisions: by making it possible for political leaders to take certain actions or by enabling others to persuade the political leaders to behave differently.

In regard to foreign policy issues, it is often said that the first role is the more common one and that the American public will go along with whatever the president decides. This may be another way of saying that most people in the United States have little interest in most foreign policy issues and prefer to leave them to the government. Support for this view comes from public opinion surveys, which have found that the proportion of respondents who agree with any given statement is usually greater if they are told that the president also agrees. (Except where otherwise indicated, these observations are based on a compilation of survey results on war/peace issues provided to the author by Hazel G. Erskine, polls editor of the Public Opinion Quarterly. Mrs. Erskine located more than 1,000 questions on such issues that were administered to national cross-sections between 1935 and 1970.)

To take an old example, in September 1941 the Gallup Poll asked a national cross-section. "Should the United States go into the war now and send an army to Europe to fight?" In response, 87 percent said "no," only 9 percent said "yes," and 4 percent were undecided. Yet in May of the same year the Gallup Poll had received quite different answers to a differently phrased question on the same issue: "If Roosevelt and our leading military experts say that Britain will be defeated unless we go into the war in the near future, would you favor, or oppose, going into the war within a few days?" When the question was put this way, enlisting governmental prestige and invoking the specter of a British defeat, 49 percent of the respondents said they would favor going to war, although 43 percent were still opposed.

A more recent example concerns the Vietnam war. In April 1968, Gallup interviewers asked: "The North Vietnamese have said that if we agree to stop the bombing, they will agree to peace negotiations. How do you feel—should we stop the bombing or not?" Despite the promise of peace negotiations, 50 percent thought the bombing should continue while 40 percent did not. A few days after this question was asked, President Johnson ordered a halt to air attacks over most of North Vietnam. Almost immediately, the Harris Poll put the following question to respondents: "Do you approve or disapprove of the President's decision to halt bombings of North Vietnam to get the Communists to start peace negotiations?" This time, 54 percent approved while 24 percent disapproved and the rest were not sure. Approximately a week later, the Gallup Poll found 64 percent of a cross-section saying they approved of the presidential decision to stop the bombing. Within the space of a few days, a presidential decision had converted a minority into a majority.

The presidential decision was, of course, itself influenced by public opinion. Poll-conscious President Johnson was aware that support for his administration's Vietnam policy was eroding. Between February and March 1968, those who described themselves as "hawks" to Gallup interviewers decreased from 60 to 41 percent, while "doves" increased from 24 to 42 percent.

This erosion of support for administration policy, which also occurred during the Korean War, demonstrates that the president does not automatically receive majority support when it comes to foreign affairs, even though his prestige is still a factor to be reckoned with. It suggests that, when influential spokesmen for opposing points of view make themselves heard by large numbers of citizens, they too can rally appreciable support. The following generalizations appear to hold, although they cannot be proved: During relatively "quiet" periods in international relations, relatively few people take an interest in foreign affairs and the noninterested majority is content to follow the government's lead. During crisis periods, if opposition leaders can gain wide attention, the "apathetic majority" tends to split into two groups—those who support the government and those who do not. The "attentive minority"—those who concern themselves with foreign affairs most of the time—is less likely to be influenced by governmental prestige or the mass media; their views tend to be more stable and to change more slowly.

If the above speculations are correct, then the backing that the government usually receives on foreign policy issues is only partially a result of presidential prestige and is also due to the fact that the government view may be the only one that receives extensive mass media coverage. When opposing views also receive wide attention in the general media, then the public may demand policy changes; both sides can mobilize public opinion.

The Vietnam case, as well as such issues as birth control and protection of the environment, illustrates that bodies of public opinion can be organized and that policy-makers then have to take them into account—even though they may not accede to them completely. Air pollution, for example, was cited as a "very serious" or "somewhat serious" problem by 28 percent of a national cross-section in 1965 and by 69 percent of those who responded to an identically worded question just five years later. (Erskine, 1972, p. 121.) Part of this increase in concern can be attributed to increasing pollution during the five-year period, but certainly not all of it. Another important explanatory factor is the increased attention given environmental problems by the mass media. That governmental leaders responded

to growing public concern is evidenced by numerous pieces of legis-
lation for the protection of the environment enacted during recent
years.

For the mass media to mobilize sentiment on an issue, there
must of course be interest in the issue and also a widespread predis-
position in favor of doing something about it. Public opinion surveys
make it clear that peace—and such related subjects as conflict resolution, arms control, and the United Nations—have consistently satisfied
these requirements. At least, poll questions asking respondents
whether they favor policies designed to ensure peace, or oppose policies
leading to war, usually elicit a majority response favorable to the
peaceful option. There are important exceptions, as when the country
is already at war or almost at war, but even these exceptions may
underline the desire for peace. That is, the opponent may be seen as
so immoral that it is necessary to crush him completely in order to
avoid a more serious war.

The following questions and responses are typical of a large
number that might be cited:

	Yes	No	Don't Know
June 1946 (Gallup): "Would you approve of the United States taking part [in a world-wide holiday set aside to promote peace and understanding]?"	74	17	9
March 1952 (NORC—National Opinion Research Center of the University of Chicago): "Do you think the U.S. should go to war against Russia now?"	12	81	7
September 1954 (NORC): "Do you think the U.S. should go to war against Russia now?"	7	88	5

In May 1957, the Gallup organization asked. "Which of these
foreign policies should our government follow: do everything possible
to prevent wars between foreign governments, even if it means threatening to fight countries which start wars, or do everything possible
to keep us out of foreign wars?" Predictably, 94 percent replied
"keep us out of wars" while 6 percent chose the alternative "prevent
war." (Free and Cantril, 1967, p. 62.) More recently, Gallup interviewers asked respondents who said they were informed about the
Middle East situation (59 percent of a national cross-section) what
they would like to see the U.S. government do about it. In 1967, a
total of 41 percent said, "stay out of the conflict," while 25 percent
advocated working for peace through the United Nations or in some
other way. Only 5 percent thought troops should be sent to support
Israel, although another 16 percent favored other forms of aid. The

rest had no opinion. Responses were similar when the same question was asked again in 1969, but the proportion saying "stay out" had risen to 52 percent while only one percent favored sending troops to the Middle East.

As far as arms control is concerned, poll results since 1937 rarely show the proportion favoring some form of international agreement to limit weapons as falling below 50 percent. During the cold war, when trust of the Soviet Union was at a low ebb, slightly fewer respondents were likely to think the United States should conclude a disarmament agreement with the Russians, but even then more than 40 percent of the respondents chose this alternative. By 1969, arms control had become a truly popular concept. When, in that year, Harris interviewers asked respondents whether they would like to see President Nixon work out a peaceful settlement on arms control with the Russians, 89 percent were in favor and 5 percent opposed. Similarly, in the same year Harris found that 47 percent of a cross-section thought the United States should concentrate on arms control rather than new missile systems, while 29 percent disagreed and the rest were not sure.

Except in rare cases, large proportions of respondents usually favor negotiations and summit conferences, whether with Hitler, Stalin, or Mao. Negotiation and compromise are appealing slogans. The United Nations, likewise, is a popular symbol. While dissatisfaction with the United Nations increased during the late 1960s and early 1970s, support has always been at a high level. As of 1967, Gallup found that 85 percent of a cross-section thought the United States should keep up its membership in the world organization, while 10 percent disagreed. In the summer of 1972, some 65 percent of the respondents approached by Minnesota poll (Minneapolis Tribune) interviewers expressed satisfaction "with the job the United Nations has done up to now" while 29 percent said they were dissatisfied. (Current Opinion, October 1972.) A slightly different type of question was administered to a national cross-section at about the same time. When asked whether the "United States should cooperate fully with the United Nations," 63 percent agreed and 28 percent disagreed. (Watts and Free, 1973, p. 200.)

One can also cite poll results that would give a very different picture of sentiment among the American public. Large majorities have usually been in favor of a strong defense establishment; they have favored wars under some conditions; they have also shown profound distrust of foreign governments. Further, people may respond to a poll question even though they have little knowledge about the issue concerned, and they may give inconsistent responses to two or more questions. The fact that poll results may change significantly with slight changes in wording indicates that opinions on some matters are lightly held.

All this is true, but the important point is not that the mass public is sometimes inconsistent and usually has little information about foreign affairs. The significant fact for our present purposes is that there is a broad reservoir of potential support for policies and proposals designed to achieve peaceful resolution of international differences. If the mass media publicize these policies, an appreciable body of public opinion can be mobilized behind them and this body of opinion will usually be taken into account by policy-makers. Majority support, as shown by the polls, is not necessary for public opinion to be a significant political factor; minority opinion may also be important especially when the majority is simply disinterested. For instance, if a political leader knows that an appreciable minority would favor a given course of action he may adopt this course, reasoning that he can rally more people to his side later.

Even when public opinion plays no role in policy decisions, governments are still dependent on the mass media when it comes to explaining their actions and gaining public cooperation. If political leaders do not have adequate mass communication facilities at their disposal or are unable to use them effectively, they are less likely to implement their policies successfully. This has not been a problem in the United States in recent times, although it was in frontier days when wars were sometimes continued because word of the peace treaty had not been received. Governments in developing countries today still find it difficult to explain their policies, whether these concern foreign affairs, agriculture, or cultural matters, to people in remote areas. The mere existence or nonexistence of mass media channels may thus affect a government's power to act.

There are, of course, many other factors that influence decisions in addition to mass communication. These include the personal predispositions of the decision-makers, the strength or weakness of their political organizations, the economic and military means at their disposal, the actions of other states, and so on. Nevertheless, the mass media enter into the decision process at a sufficient number of points to make it appear reasonable that they can often play a significant role in the avoidance of conflict or in its peaceful resolution.

4

SOME PEACE-KEEPING
ASSIGNMENTS FOR
THE MEDIA

Given that mass communication can influence behavior, even if only in certain ways and under certain conditions; and given that the mass media may enter into the political decision-making process, even if only as one of several factors; what then are the roles that mass communication might play in the advancement of international understanding?

The problem is to specify tasks that are within the limited capabilities of the mass media and that, if carried out, might contribute at least marginally to a more peaceful world. It is probable that there are a great many tasks that satisfy these two conditions, and it should be a priority concern of researchers to identify and explore as many of them as possible. At the present time, there is no way to make a systematic selection among the likely alternatives: Standard operating procedures for conflict resolution and peace-keeping have not been developed; approaches that are useful under one set of circumstances may be inappropriate under other conditions. Therefore, the best that can be done is to outline a number of tasks for mass communication that, in the light of conventional wisdom, would seem both feasible and useful in a variety of situations.

Six such tasks have been selected. They are based on the following assumptions about international relations, which admittedly do not hold in all cases: that the more information politically interested people in two or more states have about each other, the more likely these states are to resolve their differences without violence; that the more accurately and dispassionately communication can transmit messages to people in different nations, the more likely their leaders are to find ways of resolving conflicts peacefully; that the sooner political leaders give their attention to solving international differences, the less likely these differences are to lead to violence; that international conflict will be reduced in proportion to the degree and skill with which available mechanisms for the peaceful resolution of differences are used; that international agreements are more likely to be reached and respected if the public mood in the countries concerned is favorable to the conclusion and maintenance of these agreements; that political leaders are more likely to seek and find ways of resolving conflict if such action is favored by an appreciable body of opinion in their respective countries, or by international public opinion.

The six tasks for the mass media, phrased tersely and in some cases perhaps obscurely, are then as follows:

- To increase the quantity of international communication.
- To increase the quality of international communication.
- To provide early warning of situations that might lead to conflict, as well as to alert political leaders and attentive publics to opportunities for increasing international understanding.
- To stimulate the use of mechanisms for conflict resolution, such as negotiation, mediation, and arbitration, and to provide information that will tend to facilitate these processes.
- To help create a mood in which peaceful solutions are more likely to be sought and accepted.
- To mobilize, or help to establish contacts among, those who are interested in finding peaceful solutions, and to help build public opinion favoring such solutions.

These tasks will be explicated in the remainder of this chapter, and an effort will be made to show how the capabilities of mass communication might be used in their attainment.

INCREASING THE QUANTITY OF INFORMATION

Augmenting the flow of international communication will not necessarily prevent disagreement and violent conflict. Just as two well-informed people who read the same newspapers may have fundamental differences, two or more nations may know a great deal about each other and still go to war. Even a communication instrument that is designed specifically to avoid misunderstandings may be used to heighten them. Hans Speier has noted that the "hot line" between Washington and Moscow can be used to distort as well as to divulge facts and intentions (Speier, 1969, p. 1097) and more than one "good will" conference or student exchange program has ended up with a net loss of good will among the participants.

Nevertheless, a strong case can be made that, while knowledge is not necessarily a force for peace, ignorance is likely to lead to misunderstanding and conflict—it can impede necessary and prudent action and it can fail to inhibit impetuous and imprudent action. Communication breakdown, although rarely a basic cause of conflict, is one of the most common signs of impending conflict. And while restoration of communication cannot usually solve a basic disagreement by itself, it is one of the necessary preliminaries to finding a solution. We will argue, therefore, that the overall effects of increasing the flow of information among nations will be a more peaceful world. This proposition is scarcely novel. As Jerome Frank puts it, "The more complete the information people have about each other, the harder it is in general to maintain mutual hatred based on partial or distorted views." (Frank, 1968, p. 231.) He adds that if people have free access to information about other groups, normal curiosity will impel them to pay attention to it. Another authority on international communication has maintained that "conflict is a breakdown in communication and the chances of conflict increase proportionately as communication declines." (Markham, 1972, p. 31.)

Support for this position comes not only from observation of the role of communication in international relations but from experimental simulations and studies of small groups and complex organizations. When, for example, the Canadian and American Friends Service Committees jointly sponsored an "invasion" of a Canadian island in order to learn more about the role of nonviolence in resisting military force, one of the problems noted was the breakdown of communication between the occupation forces and the occupied community. (Olson and Christiansen, 1966.) Similarly, in a small group experiment exploring the relationship among trust, trustworthiness, and amount of communication, it was found that both trust and trustworthiness increased as more complete communications were sent and received. (Loomis, 1959.) Other experiments have come to similar conclusions. Psychologists have established that repeated exposure makes words more positive, food more appetizing, strangers more acceptable. Indeed, even arguing against something may make it more attractive since each mention tends to increase familiarity with it. (Zajonc, 1970.)

Studies of lateral conflict among different units or divisions within the same organization are of particular interest since these conflicts bear certain resemblances to disputes among sovereign states within the world community. The first overt sign of intra-organizational conflict often is provided by changes in the way the parties exchange information. One unit may begin to withhold certain information from another or to place limits on types of interaction, for instance, to insist that all communications be in writing.

The other unit is likely to respond in kind. Mutual suspicion and hostility result, and this has the effect of further inhibiting the flow of information and making it more difficult for the parties to cooperate. (Walton and Dutton, 1969, pp. 79-81.)

Even when intentional withholding of information does not occur, barriers to communication may contribute to inter-unit conflict within an organization. These barriers may be caused by semantic differences due to differences in training, by insufficient information channels within the organization, or by bias introduced within the channels that do exist. As a result, one unit may not know enough about the other's job to avoid making unreasonable demands on it because of sheer ignorance, it may be difficult to assign either credit or blame, and the two units may pursue disparate goals. (Walton and Dutton, 1969, p. 77.)

Whether or not insufficient communication is a cause of intra-organizational conflict, it tends to make the conflict more serious. Opening information channels may not solve the dispute but often stops the upward spiral of hostility and ignorance and makes it possible to find and deal with the cause of the conflict. A parallel with international relations is not hard to find.

An examination of recent history suggests a fairly strong relationship between war and communication breakdown and, conversely, an association between open channels of communication and good relations. Students of the outbreak of World War I have noted the overloading of communication channels linking the great powers, the failure of these powers to make their intentions clear, and selective perceptions by decision-makers. (Frank, 1968, pp. 179ff.) At the same time, as feelings of hostility deepened, direct communication between the parties to the conflict was reduced. (O. R. Hosti, 1965.) World War II offers a less clear case, in view of the well-established aggressive character of the Nazi leadership. Nevertheless, it appears unlikely that Hitler could have prepared Germany for war without the exercise of tight controls over information entering and leaving the country over a period of several years. (Sington and Weidenfeld, 1948.) The dangers of communication failure in limited war are well illustrated by the Korean conflict, in which both China and the United States made use of public communications to signal intentions to each other but both failed to interpret the signals correctly. (Whiting, 1960.)

Many of those who are actively working toward the alleviation of international tensions almost automatically argue in favor of increasing the flow of information among antagonistic nations. Thus, the participants in the seventh Strategy for Peace Conference, held under the auspices of the Stanley Foundation in 1966, suggested a series of measures to widen communications between the United States and China. This has also been a principal concern of the U.S. Arms

Control and Disarmament Agency. The tenth Strategy for Peace Conference, in 1969, reaffirmed the recommendation regarding China and pressed for an expanded exchange of information with the Soviet Union in order to build up a climate of confidence. (Stanley Foundation, 1970, pp. 14, 21, 57.) A conference of leading Japanese and Americans, sponsored by the American Assembly in 1972, urged that the press in each country improve its coverage of the other and that American news organizations encourage their correspondents to learn Japanese. (American Assembly, 1972.) Similar suggestions have been made by many bodies, official and unofficial, and have resulted in a number of private and public cultural exchange programs and international discussions and forums.

Even propaganda that one would expect to be conceived in the narrow national interest may indirectly promote international understanding, at least in some cases. After studying World War I propaganda, Harold D. Lasswell wrote, "We are witnessing the growth of a world public, and this public has arisen in part because international propaganda has both agitated and organized it." (Lasswell, 1927, p. 10.) A student of Soviet shortwave broadcast to North America found that they could have the effect of "humanizing" the Russians for American listeners. One of his respondents remarked, "All of a sudden I realized that Russia's citizens are ordinary people." Another said, "You begin to see that the Soviet Union is not a monster . . . instead they're human, as concerned with human affairs as we are. (Smith, 1970-71, pp. 548-49.)

While increasing the quantity of international communication seems likely to have an overall beneficial effect, it is particularly important to stimulate the flow of information between groups in different countries that share certain basic interests, especially an interest in international affairs. Those who pay more than passing attention to events and conditions outside their own countries make up a relatively small proportion of most populations and consist of the elites and the attentive publics. They will in any case select out from the general stream of mass communication those items that they are interested in, but the principle of economy of effort suggests that these groups be given special attention. Since published or broadcast materials on international affairs will be disregarded by a large proportion of the general public, there will be less "wastage" if these materials are directed to specialized publics.

Information exchanges among specialized international publics have been going on for many years, probably ever since the rise of national states, and at the present time they seem to offer one of the best hopes for the advancement of international understanding. For instance, the Pugwash Conferences, which have brought together private citizens and officials from nations with varying systems of government, have often led to a substantial meeting of minds. Science magazine, reporting on the nineteenth Pugwash Conference, which took place in the Soviet Union in 1969, noted a "general sense of agreement between Eastern and Western participants concerning the necessary steps which must be taken in the search for world security." (Rich, 1969, pp. 1445-46.) Among the subjects discussed at this conference were the strategic arms limitation talks, the proposed seabed arms control agreement, chemical and biological weapons, and problems of underdevelopment.

There have been many such meetings of specialized personnel in recent years. Another example is the conference of representatives of 18 European institutes for international relations that took place in Jablonna, Poland, in 1969. This group discussed security and international cooperation in Europe and arranged for continued study of these problems and an exchange of findings. (Europa Archiv, 1969, pp. 803-4.)

A different kind of specialized communication has developed among technical representatives of the various nations in the European Common Market. Over the years, these contacts have helped to create an effective supranational bureaucratic framework. (Friedrich, 1969.) Similar if less striking developments are presumably taking place wherever national states cooperate in a common endeavor. Robert C. Angell has suggested that study and teaching abroad, visiting friends in other countries, and participation in international assistance programs all tend to have a positive value for international understanding. (Angell, 1969, p. 189.)

These examples all concern person-to-person contacts rather than communication via the mass media. Nevertheless, they suggest the importance of finding common interests about which the mass media can provide information to specialized groups in different countries, and the extent to which people from different countries are motivated to pay attention to information from foreign sources about such common interests. One study has indicated, incidentally, that there is no necessary conflict between a person's identification with his own country and identification with foreign groups with which he feels he has something in common. National unity and international group solidarity are, from a psychological point of view, not mutually exclusive. Indeed, those who are more satisfied with conditions in their own nation—persons of higher status, more education, and a subjective sense of "social superiority"—are more likely to be able to identify with foreign groups that they regard as in some way similar to themselves. (Buchanan and Cantril, 1953, p. 22.)

Communication between military specialists via the mass media may be of particular importance in avoiding conflict. Following World War II, American students of military affairs—both in and out of the government—began to devote systematic attention to military thought in the Soviet Union, using the Soviet mass press and Soviet journals as primary sources. At the same time, as it later developed, Soviet military thinkers were giving close attention to American publications on strategy, deterrence, and similar subjects. Each group gained at least some appreciation of the other's viewpoint, and it can be argued that this exchange of ideas helped to prevent misunderstandings that could have led to a third general war.

Few individuals or governments disagree in principle with the idea that increased international communication is desirable, but nearly all favor the imposition of limitations on international informational exchange. In some cases these limitations are so extensive that they make a mockery of the principle. Even the United States, which regards itself as second to none in the advocacy of freedom of information, has imposed numerous restrictions, and most states are even more restrictive. (Martin, 1958.) While agreement has been reached in the United Nations on several occasions that freedom to gather, receive, and impart information regardless of frontiers is desirable, many states have been able to support this principle only when it is hedged with very broad restrictions. For instance, Article 1 of the Draft Convention on Freedom of Information, as approved by the Third Committee of the General Assembly in 1967, specifies that the exercise of this freedom is subject to:

> such necessary restrictions as are clearly defined by law
> and applied in accordance with the law in respect of:
> national security and public order; systematic dissemina-
> tion of false reports harmful to friendly relations among
> nations and of expressions inciting to war or to national,
> racial or religious hatred; attacks on founders of reli-
> gions; incitement to violence or crime; public health and
> morals; the rights, honor and reputation of others; and
> the fair administration of justice. [Van Dyke, 1970, pp.
> 18-19.]

Laws drafted in accordance with this convention could prohibit, or could be interpreted so as to prohibit, almost any information from another country.

Restrictions on freedom of information are most frequently imposed in the name of national security, which is often seen as requiring stringent limitations on communication. A paper presented at a symposium on mass media and international understanding at Ljubljana, Yugoslavia, in 1968 maintained that the ideal of "cosmopolite freedom of information" was far less important than national sovereignty: "Cosmopolitan ideas are just pure comedy." (Najman,

1969, p. 411.) The speaker added that granting freedom to a reporter to collect information could lead to the same thing as espionage since many "harmless" items, if fitted together in the same story, could represent a threat to the security of the state.

While international freedom of information is rarely attacked in such specific terms, the practice of many nations is to give every benefit of the doubt to national security and to maintain strict controls over communications, even while formally subscribing to the principle that everyone is free to gather and receive information from any source. "National security," in turn, is often interpreted to mean the security and convenience of whatever government happens to be in power.

National identity is another value that is frequently seen as conflicting with freedom of information. At the Ljubljana Symposium in 1968, speakers from smaller nations, and especially smaller developing nations, repeatedly expressed the fear that their cultures would be overwhelmed by the torrent of communications from larger, industrialized states. They pointed out, for instance, that nearly all countries were dependent for news on one of the five large international news services—Associated Press, United Press International, Reuters, Agence France-Presse, or Tass—and that in many instances small developing countries were dependent on one of the world agencies even when it came to gathering and disseminating domestic news within their own borders.

An American speaker at the symposium characterized internationalism as now practiced as "a one-way street traveled by the powerful few," and implicitly recommended censorship until smaller nations could firmly establish their cultural identities. (Schiller, 1969, p. 99.) Another American speaker took the position that the emphasis on consumption exported by the industrialized states via the mass media would work against the forced saving for construction of basic industry that was necessary in developing countries: "Any innovation of TV broadcasting, by satellite or otherwise, which tells people anything but what the policy for development calls for, must defeat that policy." (Smythe, 1969, p. 63.) Numerous studies covering many types of communications have confirmed that the flow of information is indeed heavily from industrialized states to the developing world; no parity exists. (Galtung, 1966; Caplow and Finsterbusch, 1968; Russett and Lamb, 1969.)

Preservation of national security and national identity are real problems and must be faced, but it is doubtful that the imposition of restrictions on the flow of information is the best way to solve them. As far as security is concerned, severe curtailment of informational exchange leads to at least as many threats to the nation as does relative openness: The countries that have been most insulated from the

outside world have not been spared involvement in international conflict. And inhibitions on communication automatically sacrifice the
gains in trust and understanding that can be achieved through a two-
way exchange of ideas. On balance, security is not lessened, and may
be enhanced, by keeping restrictions on international communication
to a minimum.

As for national identity, those who fear domination by foreign
communications may be misunderstanding the situation and under-
estimating the extent to which even very small societies are able to
protect their own character if they want to. The persistence of vigorous
subcultures in the United States and other industrialized societies
suggests that centralization of some mass media does not necessarily
smother cultural identity. Development of strong national information
services is a better solution to the problem of maintaining cultural
identity than restrictions on incoming information.

Nor does the the dominance of large international news services
necessarily lead to uniformity in the diet of foreign news. Differences
among news reports reflect the countries the reports are published
in much more than the agency that issues the reports. (Östgaard,
1965, p. 50.) Those services—like the Associated Press, the United
Press International, and Reuters—that depend solely on income from
users, vary the content of their news files to satisfy the interests of
their customers in other countries. (Kruglak, 1957, p. 17.) By choosing
among the Western news agencies, Tass, the Chinese Hsin Hua (which
offers news and features in many parts of the world), and regional
agencies, the mass media in almost any country can compile a news
file to suit a wide variety of tastes.

When it comes to entertainment materials, it is a fact that mass
audiences almost everywhere seem to like a diet of a low cultural level,
largely imported from the United States, although this is no longer
true of films. Some countries have restricted the volume of these
imports, or have attempted to shut them out altogether, but this does
not seem to have prevented the growth of demand for consumer goods.
Again, censorship threatens potential gains in international understanding without conferring corresponding benefits.

Still, the demand of smaller countries for some form of "parity"
in international communications is a reasonable one. Equalization
of the flow of information across national boundaries is a goal toward
which the stronger powers as well as the weaker ones should strive.
For unless informational exchange is truly two-way, there is no real
communication. Increased quantity is likely to lead to greater international understanding if there is also increased "parity."

IMPROVING THE QUALITY OF COMMUNICATION

By "quality" we refer to the degree to which communication accurately transmits meaning from one person or society to another. Low-quality communications can easily be misunderstood or may transmit no meaning at all; high-quality messages are precise and allow the receiver, if he wishes, to ascertain almost exactly the ideas the sender intended to transmit. Few communications are of perfect quality, but some transmit meaning much better than others.

If communication is two-way, if there is a give and take, quantity in itself tends to improve quality. The receiver may misunderstand the first time and may indicate this by his response. The sender then amplifies or clarifies his meaning, and fairly accurate mutual understanding is eventually achieved.

But most international communication through the mass media is far from perfect two-way communication. The United States responds to the Soviet Union, or to Ghana, or to Costa Rica, not only on the basis of what individuals or governments in those countries do or say but also on the basis of the selection and interpretation by the mass media of what is done or said. Thus the media may present different pictures of the same situation to different audiences—and may also present inaccurate pictures to all. And the feedback mechanism, whereby misunderstandings can be corrected, is long, complicated, and often inoperative. The remarks of a U.S. political figure may be misunderstood in the Middle East, but this breakdown in communication may go unreported and uncorrected; the same is true of the remarks of a Middle Eastern political leader as reported in the United States.

The inability of the mass media to provide true two-way communication is not mainly the result of intent, at least in countries where the press is relatively free; it results from a combination of structural factors that are extremely difficult to overcome—limited capacity, limited budget, and so on. (Östgaard, 1965, pp. 39ff.)

While selection and interpretation are absolutely essential in international reporting and cannot be dispensed with, their biasing effects can be mitigated in several ways. One of these is to provide increased opportunities for checking on the meaning actually transmitted by reports from other countries. For example, during the days when debates about the proposed European Defense Community were causing heated comment in both France and West Germany, the International Press Institute enlisted the cooperation of a group of French journalists and another of German newspapermen and let them see how each country was being represented in the press of the other. Members of both groups were dismayed at the picture of their own country they found in the other country's press, and they subsequently attempted to guard against such distortions in their own coverage. (Davison, 1965, p. 24.)

Another way of partially guarding against bias introduced by selectivity and interpretation is to give others maximum opportunity to present their own case. This means using more direct quotations and giving spokesmen from one country direct access to the mass media in another. International television may provide greater opportunity for this kind of exchange than has existed in the past, especially if adequate, low-cost means of simultaneous translation are developed.

A further advantage of encouraging this kind of direct, first-person exchange is that it helps give all parties concerned greater assurance that their views are being adequately presented. One of the principal complaints of minority groups in the United States about their coverage in American mass media, when their views have been presented at all, has been that others are usually talking about them; they have been given little opportunity to reach a mass public themselves. Even the best-intentioned majority reporters or commentators, they feel, cannot give an adequate picture of the conditions under which minority groups live, and how they react to those conditions.*

Whether reports from another country are presented directly or through mass media third parties, a host of semantic problems remains. Translation nearly always involves some compromise with meaning; even if translation is as accurate as possible, the connotations of words, their significance for different audiences, may differ appreciably.

The word "peace," for instance, refers in some cultures to a state of mind, in others to a condition of harmony in the social order, and in still others to a just relationship. (Takeshi, 1969.) The word "ghetto" has different connotations in Western Europe, where it refers to the enforced residence of the Jewish community in a given part of a city; in the United States, where it is applied to a depressed urban area inhabited by any minority; and in the Arab Middle East, where it is thought of as the stronghold of an "aggressive alien minority." (Abu Bakr, 1969, p. 279.)

---

*These observations are based primarily on an unpublished pilot study of minority group coverage in the New York press, undertaken by the Graduate School of Journalism and the Bureau of Applied Social Research of Columbia University in 1969. In general, it is surprising how little effort has been devoted to applying research on minority groups in the United States and elsewhere to problems of international relations. This remains a fertile field for scholarship.

Indeed, it has been suggested that current political terminologies are inadequate because they can be used to convey such a variety of meanings, and that a new language more adequate to man's real needs should be constructed. (Werkheiser, 1968a and b.) Students have also pointed out that, as well as attaching different meanings to the same words, people from different cultures employ different styles of thought: Some prefer to reason from the general to the particular, while others favor inductive reasoning. (Glenn, 1954.)

Much has been written about semantic difficulties in international communication, and few are completely unaware of them. The problem remains as to how they can be minimized. One commonsense approach is for those whose words come to the attention of foreign audiences to be aware that they may be misunderstood and to guard against this by securing as much feedback as possible. It is also possible that some audiences, at least elite audiences, could be educated to be more sensitive to different styles of thought and to the various meanings that may be attached to the same word by people in different cultures. A third approach is to build a strong group of expert interpreters: Those who are completely familiar with two or more cultures and can translate not only from one language to another but from one thought system to another. All three approaches are being used, to varying degrees and with varying success, by those concerned with international communication.

One relatively simple measure that could be adopted to improve the quality of informational exchange among nations would be to avoid using political terms that are extremely vague or that are known to be subject to very different interpretations. Or, if used, such terms should be carefully defined. Ralph White has demonstrated, for instance, that "socialism" has quite a different meaning to Europeans and Americans. To most Americans, it means government ownership of industry and domination of the individual by the state. To most Europeans, it means a concern for social welfare, aid to the poor, and medical and retirement benefits—an approach Americans tend to see as quite compatible with "capitalism." (White, 1966.)

"Communism," when applied equally to the form of government in Yugoslavia and China, is also a confusing term, as are "imperialism," "neo-colonialism," and many other "isms." Use of these expressions without further definition automatically makes meaning obscure and lowers the quality of communication. When they are used as epithets there is probably little intention to convey meaning and their use is at least understandable, but they have limited use in rational discourse. Their elasticity is emphasized by a content analysis of speeches by President John F. Kennedy and Premier Nikita Khrushchev: The analysts found that Kennedy associated communism with imperialism and aggression while Khrushchev associated capitalism with imperialism and aggression. Yet both argued in favor of much the same values. (Eckhardt and White, 1967.) A former U.S. under-secretary of state has spoken of the difficulty of finding ways the United States and the Soviet Union can live together in peace and develop their common interests as long as complex realities are concealed beneath simplistic slogans. (Ball, 1969.)

In theory, it would not be difficult to abandon these "simplistic slogans." In practice, it is likely to be very difficult. Not only are they convenient and well entrenched in political vocabularies but they account for part of the political capital of politicians in various countries.

As an example of a much-used term that frequently obscures meaning, one may take the seemingly inoffensive word "people." In the context of international relations, this word often implies that there are no differences of opinion within a given population: "The people of country X welcome the generous gesture of country Y." Hitler degraded the term by phrasing his demands in terms of the desires or needs of "the German people." Leaders of many other countries, not all of them totalitarian, have done the same. When one looks at the preamble to the American Constitution, one finds the expression: "We the people of the United States. . ." Actually, those who composed and ratified this document, however meritorious, were a small group elected by rather narrow suffrage. When used by political figures, the word "people" can usually be translated to mean "government" or those in a given country who happen to agree with a given speaker.

Some exaggerated or inaccurate expressions are part of each culture and are almost automatically discounted or reinterpreted by those who know the culture well enough. It has been claimed, for instance, that a degree of puffery in American advertising is not misleading because everyone recognizes it for what it is. The same is true in American politics. As a manufacturer accused of misleading advertising said, "If I wrote the Federal Government and asked them to document the statement, 'In God We Trust,' as advertised on our currency, I wonder what sort of answer I would get." (Dougherty, 1971.) It would be impossible to eliminate all inaccurate expressions from international discourse, but at least their potentialities for causing misunderstanding could be taken into account.

A problem that is less severe as far as the quality of international communication is concerned is the use of value-laden terms to describe certain persons, groups, or movements. An Arab speaker at the Ljubljana Symposium complained that Palestinian guerrillas were being referred to in the Western press as criminals and terrorists when they should be recognized as heroes. (Abu Bakr, 1969, pp. 276ff.) (Actually, it would seem best to find neutral terms for identifying the men and women in question.) Similar complaints might be made with respect to American terms of reference to South Vietnamese who took up arms against the Saigon government, and to North Vietnamese references to the Saigon forces. Value-laden designations, sometimes epithets, do not obscure meaning the way ambiguous terms and slogans do, since it is usually fairly clear to what they refer, but they do lower the quality of international discourse by offending certain parties and making it more difficult for them to respond in terms of the real issues involved. Again, elimination of such designations and epithets would not be easy, and would pose problems for headline writers as well as for politicians.

Both slogans and value-laden designations belong, in part at least, to a broader category of devices that tend to simplify what may in fact be extremely complex situations, and thus help to prevent communications from conveying a truer picture of meaning and reality. Other devices in this category include stereotyping, lumping together all members of one group or all citizens of one nation as though they had no individual differences, and ascribing presumed motives rather than determining what the motives actually are.

One of the first tasks of communication in international relations is to destroy monolithic images and open ways for like-minded people in different states to relate to each other. It is as unrealistic to lump together all Israelis or all Arabs as it is to group all Americans or all Soviet citizens. Yet this is often done, in the supposed interest of simplicity and brevity.

The quality of a body of communications on any given subject is increased if all principal viewpoints are expressed and events are described from all sides. A resolution passed by the Ljubljana Symposium on Mass Media and International Understanding, after condemning violations of freedom of expression, expressed regret that in so many nations public opinion can see only one side of any given conflict in the world today. (Mass Media and International Understanding, 1969, p. 419.) More specifically, a news executive at a conference on television news coverage sponsored by the International Broadcast Institute noted the difficulty of giving adequate coverage to the Vietnam war when it was possible to report from one side only. He asked, "Has the effect of this monocular vision been sufficiently evaluated? How does it bear on the way in which the war is felt and understood?" (International Broadcast Institute, March 1970.) Coverage of all views and from all sides is clearly impossible in many cases, but it is an objective worth striving for.

Increasing the quality and quantity of communications will not solve the underlying causes of conflict; indeed, in some cases these causes may receive greater salience as a result of more accurate perceptions on both sides. To "have" nations, security will still mean protecting their riches, while to "have not" nations security will mean power great enough to force a more equal distribution of the wealth. But communications can help to inhibit the false images and stereotypes that have been widely recognized as an ingredient in the spiral leading to war. (Wright, 1968, p. 464.) Fuller knowledge of others tends to work against self-delusion, as in the thought process described by William Buchanan and Hadley Cantril: "Those people threaten us, they have fought against us, they are just across our border, we cannot understand what they say, hence they must be cruel, conceited, domineering, etc." (Buchanan and Cantril, 1953, pp. 57-58.) Full and accurate communication can at least keep things from looking worse than they really are. If communication cannot eliminate conflict of interest, it can reduce "conflict of understanding." (Glenn et al., 1970.)

EARLY WARNING

The time to stop an international conflict, like a fire, is before it rages out of control. This principle is widely recognized but not always applied. Governments, being composed of human beings, are prone to wait and see, to hope that if the monster is not faced he will quietly go away. Lincoln Bloomfield observes that, for overworked statesmen, "there is never a good time to plan ahead, always a good time to let sleeping dogs lie." (Bloomfield, 1966, p. 679.) He observes that, as of the time he wrote, there were at least half a dozen "dormant" disputes in the world that could flare up into violent conflict at almost any point. Yet, as long as the guns were silent, attention tended to wander elsewhere. If statesmen are to face up to difficult and dangerous situations they, like the rest of us, have to be nudged, and nudged repeatedly.

Edward Hambro, former permanent representative of Norway to the United Nations, expressed a somewhat similar idea when he observed that U.N. personnel often became aware of international problems only when they had already become critical conflicts. "We do not have the intelligence machinery necessary to prepare in advance for a reasonable solution of the problems," he said. "The agenda is so crowded that all but the most urgent problems are put aside." Hambro also referred to the necessity for outside pressure on political leaders: "We need . . . leaders of public opinion who can force statesmen and politicians into action before it is too late." (Stanley Foundation, 1972.)

Nudging, as it happens, is one of the things the mass media do best. When a situation is in the headlines, there is pressure on the powers-that-be to act on it. The press has the capability of serving as a fairly efficient early warning system, even though current limitations of personnel, news capacity, and budget keep it from fully exercising this capability. The big story of the moment tends to squeeze out stories about situations that are only potentially dangerous, and the very thin coverage of the world by international reporters makes it difficult for the press, unaided, to identify incipient conflicts.

These limitations on the press can be overcome, at least in part, through the cooperation of other kinds of organizations. Concerned groups can help to provide a continuing flow of information that will keep attention focused on threats to the peace until something is done about them. In this respect, the press itself must be stimulated. Students of international affairs, for example, can help to identify dangerous situations and call them to the attention of the press. Various ways in which this might be done will be suggested in the following chapter.

Social scientists and students of international relations can assist the press in performing an even more difficult function that is closely related to early warning. This is to point out the probable consequences of resorting to violence. As Fred C. Iklé found in his study of the way wars end, political and military leaders often fail to look beyond the first phases of conflict; they see only chances of success and do not consider the full impact of war or the consequences that might ensue if their plans go awry. He concludes that expectations regarding the outcome must take into account that the cumulative price of war may be greater than the present price for peace, and that these expectations must govern all the decisions and dynamics through which military violence might be unleashed. (Iklé, 1971, p. 108.) One way of affecting expectations of decision-makers is for the mass media to bring to their attention information and viewpoints of which they might otherwise remain only dimly aware.

CONFLICT RESOLUTION

Most conflicts that are settled peacefully are resolved as the result of some kind of negotiation, mediation, arbitration, or adjudication. Publicity has been widely regarded as the enemy of all these processes. The diplomat and the mediator usually attempt to preserve secrecy, and they prefer to keep outside pressures at arm's length until an agreement has been reached. The courts, similarly, resent what they regard as interference by the press in judicial proceedings. Juries, or even a judge, may be biased by pre-trial publicity.

It would be possible to argue that the proper role for the mass media, when international disputes are being negotiated, mediated, or adjudicated, would be to remain silent—to refrain from interfering.

This may indeed prove the preferable course of action in some cases, but we will not advocate it as a general rule for two reasons. First, surprisingly little thought has been given to the positive functions that mass communication might play in connection with these processes, although the negative implications of publicity have been dealt with extensively. There may be an extremely important role for the mass media that has simply been overlooked, and much more research on this question is called for. Second, even in the present state of knowledge there appear to be a number of ways communications can play a positive, if indirect, part in the settlement of international disputes through negotiation, mediation, arbitration, or adjudication. Publicity can help pave the way for these processes; on occasion it can make the tasks of the parties involved somewhat easier; and it can facilitate acceptance of the agreements or judgments that are reached.

A major function of communications in activating one of the mechanisms for peaceful solutions is to issue reminders that these mechanisms are available, that they have been used successfully in the past, and that they might be applicable in the present. (A study of 47 attempts to settle serious international conflicts through negotiation between 1920 and 1965 found that almost exactly half these attempts were successful—K. Holsti, 1966.) While diplomats and politicians already are aware of the availability of various avenues for settling disputes, reminders from the mass media will make it more likely that they will be explored. That such reminders might be useful is suggested by the fact that the possibility of ending the war in Vietnam by adjudication—that is, by referring it to the International Court of Justice—received little attention. (Holton, 1968.) And on several occasions national representatives in the United Nations have proposed investigations to determine why existing institutions for the settlement of international disputes were not used more often. (Bailey, 1971, p. 40.)

The mass media can contribute toward the success of negotiations by helping to ensure that each side is truly familiar with the other's position. Students of bargaining and negotiation have often noted the degree to which each party misunderstands, or unintentionally distorts, what the other side is saying. This distortion may come about as a result of bureaucratic processes or unconscious psychological processes. A psychologist, referring to these internal barriers to understanding, has called negotiation a "dialogue of the deaf." (Stagner, 1967, pp. 161-62.) To overcome this deafness, some social scientists have advocated as a ground rule for all negotiations "that there be no bargaining until the parties could express each others' positions to their mutual satisfaction." (Frank, 1968, p. 222.) Negotiations are also facilitated if each side can visualize the circumstances under which the other's position might be valid and can recognize similarities between the other and the self. (Rapoport, 1964, pp. 175-76.) The ability of at least the prestige press to cut through the layers of bureaucracy that filter information for both governments and negotiators makes it an instrument that might significantly help in bringing each side's position home to the other.

If each side in a dispute is willing to acknowledge publicly and in its own media that it understands the position of the other side, even while not sharing it, agreement is likely to be facilitated. This is suggested by an analysis of editorials in the elite newspapers of India and Pakistan during their conflict in 1965 over the Rann of Kutch and Kashmir. (Rao, 1972, esp. p. 161.) Such public acknowledgment of the opponent's position may hasten effective communication between the parties involved. It may also help to prevent either side from allowing its own position to become a slogan that is automatically and self-righteously repeated without reexamination.

Through mass communications new alternatives may be called to the attention of negotiators and their governments. These may come from third countries or from private citizens in the countries concerned. Case studies have indicated that political leaders often fail to explore alternatives to a course of action on which they have decided and may subconsciously distort information that weighs against their policies; indeed, some alternatives may become too painful for them to face. (Iklé, 1971, pp. 16, 95-105.) The press may serve as a powerful reminder that other alternatives exist.

At the least, mass communication channels can help to ensure that all parties to a negotiation, or a conflict, have as large a pool of shared information as possible. This does not mean that the importance of national goals will be diminished, but at least it may avoid some of the misunderstandings caused by the fact that different parties are focusing their attention on different aspects of the situation.

While interagency relations do not offer a precise parallel to international relations, studies of the role of information in interagency cooperation and conflict are highly suggestive. Richard E. Walton observes, on the basis of an examination of a number of interagency projects, that all of them suffered from lack of shared information. Each agency representative relied on his own sources, with the result that each tended to be suspicious of others who had a different set of facts at their disposal. Walton concludes that "information systems must play a key role in enhancing the effectiveness of interagency project management in general and conflict resolution in particular." (Walton, 1969, p. 22.)

When it comes to mediation, mass communications can make the mediator's task somewhat easier through their ability to confer prestige. Students of intra-organizational conflict have found that third persons who intervene should be of relatively high influence and perceived expertise. (Walton and Dutton, 1969, pp. 79-80.) Even though a mediator's prestige in his own country will depend largely on his position and past achievements, his prestige in the world as a whole will depend mainly on how he is treated by the international press. The importance of the mediator's function can also be emphasized— that a third-party helper is often needed in conflict resolution if either side is to realize at least some of its objectives. (Lippitt, 1970.)

On occasion, the press may be able to bring to the attention of the mediator useful items of information he would not otherwise know about. Those who have mediated international disputes have reported that their chances of talking with nongovernmental people and hearing things the disputing governments did not want them to hear were sometimes very limited. (Carnegie Endowment for International Peace, 1969, p. 44.) It is possible that public channels can be used to inform mediators when it would be impolitic for them to seek out their own sources of information. Also, public coverage of a negotiation may facilitate agreement among negotiators if public opinion generally favors it. This was the case with respect to the European Economic Community, and the EEC Commission was able to reinforce its mediation efforts by building up a feeling of impatience about unsettled disputes. As a last resort, a mediator may threaten to make his recommendations public, thus exposing the intransigence of the party that rejected them. (Carnegie Endowment for International Peace, 1969, p. 28, 30.)

The mass media can also assist the mediator by emphasising what have been called "mediatory values." These are values that may help to compensate or reward one or both parties for making concessions. (Edmead, 1971, pp. 35-38.) They include the norms of behavior expected of members of the international community—a preference for peaceful solutions, respect for international law, and compliance with the U.N. Charter and U.N. resolutions. They also include the kinds of behavior suggested by religions, ideologies, or traditions, or behavior suggested by prior agreements and preferred methods for settling disputes. Thus, national representatives may feel more secure in giving up at least part of their demands if these concessions can be justified in terms of adherence to past promises, their nation's traditional magnanimity, the ideals of the dominant religion, or the conviction that such matters should be settled by the International Court of Justice or by a plebiscite. The more the mass media use their capabilities to focus attention on these values and to confer prestige on them, the easier it is for a mediator—or even the negotiating parties—to appeal to them in justifying compromise solutions.

All forms of conflict resolution can, through the press, become important educational influences, and acceptance of agreements or decisions arrived at will be more likely if this education takes place. J. David Singer has advocated, for instance, that disarmament talks be "open," pointing out that the major parties can still meet in secret if they want to and that, even if one side is more interested in propaganda than negotiation, third parties will learn from the proceedings. (J. D. Singer, 1968, p. 197.)

Agreements, once reached, are more likely to be observed and remembered if the press is able to keep attention focused on them. As the Soviet author Alexandr Solzhenitzyn (1972) has observed, although in a different context, "suppression of information renders international signatures and agreements illusory . . . it costs nothing to reinterpret any agreement, even simpler—to forget it, as though it has never existed."

CREATING A MOOD HOSPITABLE TO PEACEFUL SOLUTIONS

The greatest contribution of mass communications to the peaceful resolution of some conflicts is likely to come from their ability to influence the moods of governments, elites, attentive publics, and general publics. We are using the term "mood" here to refer both to the totality of attitudes relevant to international relations and to the complexes of attitudes relevant to various aspects of international relations. A general mood is represented by the feeling that there will always be war, or the feeling that permanent peace is possible. A more specific mood might apply only to relations between two specific nations.

Whether negotiation, mediation, or arbitration will be undertaken depends in part on the moods of governments and elites. Whether the results of peace-making efforts will be accepted depends heavily on the moods of attentive publics and sometimes mass publics as well.

Moods, both general and specific, are even more important for informal, day-to-day international negotiations and discussions than they are when these processes become formalized and publicized. The peaceful settlement of existing or potential conflicts among nations takes place constantly in all capitals and at the United Nations, often as a result of informal conversations, or even telephone calls, among diplomats. If the feeling between two countries is good, rather serious differences may be resolved in this manner. If the feeling is poor, minor frictions may escalate into major conflicts. With reference to the Berlin blockade in 1948, when the Soviet Union and East Germany cut the land routes between West Germany and West

Berlin, an American diplomat subsequently remarked that if a dispute of this nature had arisen with the British it could have been resolved informally, although it would have been difficult, but with the Russians this was impossible. Clearly he was referring to the difference in the atmosphere between the United States and Great Britain, on the one hand, and the United States and the Soviet Union, on the other.

Mass communications can be most effective in influencing specific attitudes and general moods during periods when international tension is relatively low—when there are few crises and alarms and when emotions are not running high. At such times, the media's capacity to create new attitudes is greatest and they can activate and reinforce states of mind hospitable to the settlement of specific differences as well as to the creation and strengthening of institutions for the peaceful resolution of disputes in general. In international relations, as in farming, the time to make hay is while the sun shines.

More specifically, the mass media should foster a state of mind in which peaceful solutions, even to seemingly intractable and enduring conflicts, are accepted as conceivable and possible, and in which a person who works for a utopia does not have to apologize for being soft-headed. Such a state of mind of acceptance has been brought about in the last few decades with respect to science. It is no longer fashionable to label even the most extreme predictions of scientific achievement as "impossible," whereas earlier a common stereotype was that of the mad scientist peddling "unrealistic dreams"—such as manned flight or transmission of messages through the airwaves. Actual scientific achievements have been the major factor in changing this stereotype, but mass communications, and especially journalistic writing about science, have played no small role. The media have been even more important in convincing many citizens of developing countries that their vision of living in an industrialized society is attainable. They can conceive of themselves as adopting a totally new way of life. (Lerner, 1958, p. 400.) And once the possibility is acknowledged, the road to realization is open, even though the way may be a long one. Images of a world at peace can perform a similar function.

Conceptions of ways violent conflict could be avoided are advanced every year, but by and large they receive little attention from the mass media. There is, for instance, the vision of a peaceful world arrived at through common motivations of all peoples, the idea of a "global safety system" in which the military establishments of all countries would cooperate, or the more limited proposal for collaboration between the North Atlantic Treaty Organization and the Warsaw Pact countries in keeping the peace in Europe. (H. G. and H. B. Kurtz, 1969; Brzezinski, 1968). Greater attention to these utopias, some of which no longer look so difficult of achievement, would lead to more such proposals and to better consideration of those that are advanced.

The atmosphere in which peaceful solutions can be achieved will also be promoted by the mass media if they are able to emphasize common values: the aspects of life that unite rather than divide two or more states. One student of international relations has recommended that the United States seek common ground with its opponents and publicly accept as much of their point of view as possible. He sees a number of areas in which American values overlap with those of the Soviet Union: for instance, respect for scientific achievement, preference for small-unit ownership, and commitment to a social welfare system. (White, 1969.) In this connection, it is probable that American recognition of Soviet scientific advances and Soviet recognition of similar advances in the United States have helped to improve the atmosphere in which arms control negotiations between the two nations have been conducted.

Those who espouse a "convergence theory"—that the Soviet and some other communist systems are becoming more similar to the systems in the United States and Western Europe, while the latter are also beginning to resemble the former in some respects—also tend to emphasize common values. (Sullivan, 1969.) The convergence theory has detractors (Leontiev, 1968) as well as prominent advocates in the various countries concerned, but insofar as it is accepted—and publicized—it works in favor of a more benign mood in East-West relations.

Emphasizing the importance of common values in somewhat different terms, participants in the tenth annual Strategy for Peace Conference concluded:

> Finally, it is urged that both the United States and the U.S.S.R. accept the fact that certain fundamental internal differences between them are not likely to be overcome easily and may endure for a long time. The two powers, therefore, should seek agreements where their interests coincide instead of stressing those differences as stumbling blocks to negotiations or as excuses for failing to make progress in the SALT [Strategic Arms Limitation Talks]. [Stanley Foundation, 1970.]

As the above quotation suggests, emphasis on common values does not mean ignoring differences. Instead, it suggests using parallel interests as a springboard for action rather than referring to existing differences as justification for doing nothing.

Even when two or more states share few values, they may still trust each other, and the mass media can contribute substantially toward establishing trust—which is an essential component of a mood favoring peaceful resolution of disagreements. Indeed, distrust has been called the greatest enemy of disarmament. (Frank, 1968, pp.

193ff.) Communications can dwell either on the reliability or the un-reliability of another party. To the extent that they give disproportion-ate attention to cases in which agreements have been violated, they cultivate distrust. When they present a faithful accounting of agree-ments observed and agreements violated by both sides, they contribute toward trust as much as circumstances permit. Unfortunately, the tendency has been for the mass media, as well as people in general, to permit one violation to obscure many cases of observance.

Mass communications are likely to contribute toward a stable, trusting relationship when they portray both parties as having equal power. In the words of a research report prepared for the U.S. Arms Control and Disarmament Agency, "attributing either power inferiority or superiority to the adversary tends to make one's trust toward the adversary unstable," and "the specific policy orientation that comprises a favorable climate for negotiating and implementing an arms control agreement is more likely to be found under perceived parity than either superiority or inferiority." (Walton et al., January 1969, p. 41.) This would suggest that the practice of many Americans of referring to the United States as the most powerful country in the world is a destructive one, as far as a mood conducive to international agreements is concerned. And the statement is also misleading, since power in the United States is so widely shared that under some cir-cumstances the government's ability to act is severely limited. While relative degrees of national power do exist and must sometimes be acknowledged, it would appear conducive to an atmosphere of inter-national trust if they were not emphasized in public communications.

Trust ordinarily tends to increase with increased volume of communication between two parties, but it increases more rapidly if both parties make clear their intentions, their expectations as to how the other will respond, and what they will do if the other party does not respond as expected. Will a penalty be imposed on him or will he be allowed another chance? (J. L. Loomis, 1959; Osgood, 1962.) In general, the more frank and open a communication, the more likely it is to increase trust.

As common sense would suggest, the mass media contribute toward a favorable mood for conflict resolution when they avoid a tone of crisis, which can activate and reinforce the latent fears pre-sent in any government and population. When an individual is under high stress, he is less able to assimilate complex communications and he tends to consider fewer policy alternatives. This generaliza-tion appears to apply to both governments and publics. (Walton et al., January 1969, p. 11; Walton, September 1968, p. 53.) Ability to utilize information most effectively occurs at a moderate stress level, where the seriousness of the situation is apparent but where it is not per-ceived as a crisis. A sense of crisis also tends to make people look for more information to justify their fears and promotes polarization of attitudes, thus contributing to the spiral leading to violent conflict. (Coleman, 1957.)

These observations about the negative effects of a crisis atmosphere are derived largely from the experimental literature of social psychology, but they receive support from case studies of actual crisis situations. (W. L. Gould, 1968.)

It is very difficult for the commercial mass media, at least, to avoid playing a part in creating a crisis atmosphere. To make a threat is a very reliable technique for securing attention in politics, and when politicians use this device the press has to report the threats that are made. At the same time, a story reporting a threat is usually regarded as an important one, and reporters have little motivation to discount the threat or report additional information that would make the threat appear less serious. (Strickland, 1968.) The temptation for the press to play up a "scare" story is strong. A student of the United Nations has observed that the ease and speed of modern communication is one reason for the prevalence of a crisis atmosphere in U.N. circles. He asks, "If technological advances can be used to cause and exacerbate conflict, can they not also be used to ameliorate it?" (Bailey, 1971, p. 23.)

MOBILIZING THOSE CONCERNED WITH INTERNATIONAL UNDERSTANDING

One of the most easily demonstrable capabilities of mass communications is their ability to bring like-minded people together, to coordinate their actions, to help organizations to form, and to facilitate the growth of public opinion. To date, this capability has been used more effectively in mobilizing populations for war than in rallying those who are interested in finding peaceful solutions.

There are numerous practical difficulties standing in the way of utilizing communications to mobilize those who wish to promote international understanding. One is the complexity of the concept of "peace" and the large number of ways it can be defined. It can be argued—and has been—that almost any action or program is in the interest of peace; "peace" is a value almost everyone claims to favor. An additional problem is the tendency of those engaged in promoting international comity to organize their activities around certain specific objectives or formulas, which may or may not be shared by many other people. As of the early 1960s there were about 1,500 groups around the world that represented themselves as working for disarmament and peace, most of them rather weak. (Galtung, 1968, p. 495.) The ability of these groups to cooperate has not been impressive.

48

Added to the diversity of their immediate objectives is the tendency of many of them to feel that they have a monopoly on truth and that those who favor other paths to international understanding are in the camp of the enemy.

Therefore, communications originated by peace groups often tend to be divisive. A fund-raising appeal distributed by the U.S. branch of the World Federalists (WFUSA) in 1970, for instance, included the following appeal: "WFUSA is actively engaged in building a peace constituency to confront the war machine. We need your help." Such an appeal would be likely to repel any who believe that at the present time national military establishments are necessary to preserve peace, even though they might also favor some kind of world federation.

Similarly, a pamphlet published by the Friends Peace Committee in 1969 warned that specialists in peace-keeping had not taken into sufficient account the rapid obsolescence of the military as an appropriate instrument for organizing peace. (Walker, 1969, p. 20.) The statement may or may not be true, but it could scarcely be expected to promote cooperation with the many men in uniform who have served with U.N. peace-keeping forces or who sincerely believe that the military profession can contribute toward the achievement of a more peaceful world in other ways.

And a "World Conference on Vietnam" that met in Stockholm in 1967 under the sponsorship of a number of peace organizations ended by repelling as many of those who were potentially interested as it attracted. It excluded the militant Vietnamese Buddhists, its revolutionary emphasis kept away moderate anti-war representatives, and its failure to produce explicit procedural rules hampered the inclusion of minority dissent. (Jack, 1967.)

To be used successfully to mobilize people who seek peaceful solutions to international disputes, communications must follow somewhat the same guidelines as when they are used to promote agreements among nations; that is, they must emphasize points of agreement and attempt to promote action on these, without ignoring differences of opinion. The media can play a useful part in stimulating negotiations among groups with differing programs and priorities, in the hope that a larger and larger common ground can be found. The ultimate aim, as far as rallying partisans of international understanding is concerned, is to find positions that can be accepted by the doctrinaire pacifist, the professional military officer, and all those in between. To the extent that at least some common values can be identified, mass communications can help to coordinate action by groups having rather diverse views.

The mass media can help to bring together people in different nations, as well as in the same nation, and can promote the formation and growth of like-minded groups, formal organizations, and world public opinion. William Evan has proposed, for example, that at some future time the United Nations might provide a forum for individual citizens from many countries as well as for governments. (Evan, 1962.) The potential role of international communication in the creation of such organizations is obvious. While some states attempt to enforce uniformity of opinion on their citizens, making cross national ties difficult except through official channels, these policies are not immune to change. A speaker at the Ljubljana Symposium noted that various nations in the communist world were allowing greater freedom of communication: that differentiated public opinion was emerging, a kind of opinion pluralism; and that these opinions were a factor that influenced the governing process. (Vreg, 1969, p. 43.)

It appears likely that mass communication can increasingly bind like-minded groups in various countries together, making them a force on the international political scene. Indeed, Alexandr Solzhenitsyn (1972) attributed preservation of his freedom in part to pressure exerted by the international community of writers: "During my dangerous weeks of exclusion from the Writers Union, the wall of defense advanced by the world's prominent writers protected me from worse persecutions. . . ."

There are certainly other ways the mass media could help to reduce violent conflict and promote international understanding. Since communication is involved in all social processes, and since a large proportion of these processes have a bearing on war and peace, the possibilities are almost infinite. We believe, however, that the six tasks discussed above are among the most promising avenues along which progress could be made. Besides, they are enough to keep us busy.

5

POTENTIAL CONTRIBUTIONS
BY THE MEDIA

Assuming that the objectives described in Chapter 4 are worthwhile, the question is how to work toward them through the instrumentalities of mass communication. All media have potentialities and limitations; there are certain rules they must of necessity obey. Commercial media must make a profit if they are to survive. Government-operated channels must conform to the requirements of the political system of which they are a part. Private, nonprofit media are likely to suffer from underfinancing. The communication facilities of the United Nations not only have very limited budgets but are subject to conflicting pressures from the member-states.

Nevertheless, each of these instrumentalities enjoys some leeway. There are certain things they are doing that they could afford to stop doing; there are other things they are not doing that they could undertake. All of them can contribute in various ways to the goals of peace-making and peace-keeping and are already doing so. If all their potentialities were used more fully, even more substantial progress toward these goals could be made.

The analysis and suggestions that follow are based primarily on the situation in the United States, although in some cases they may apply in other countries also. Of course, communication facilities in different parts of the world have varying characteristics, so each media system can best contribute toward common goals in its own manner. It is to be hoped that scholars in other nations will review the characteristics and capabilities of their own mass media in a similar search for ways they could make a larger contribution to international understanding.

In the United States, the private newspaper press, radio, magazines, and television dominate the channels of communication. They bring the bulk of the news to which the population gives its attention, and they bring it first. They also provide most of the background and interpretive comment against which the news is judged. Seemingly, in order to increase the quantity and quality of information about other countries, to provide early warning of dangerous situations, to facilitate peaceful settlement of international disputes, to mobilize those interested in working toward international understanding, and to promote a mood favorable to conflict resolution, all that would be necessary would be to enlist the cooperation of the private media.

This, however, is a simplistic view, reflecting popular misconceptions about the power and functions of the press. As Walter Lippmann noted in 1922, there is a tendency in democracies to load the responsibility for curing social ills on the press, to expect it to succeed where government and other institutions have failed. In Lippmann's words, "It is too frail to carry the whole burden of popular sovereignty, to supply spontaneously the truth which democrats hoped was inborn." (Lippmann, 1922, p. 273.)

Furthermore, the commercial press is already a self-critical institution and, while conforming to the economic requirements of the marketplace, is populated by groups of professionals whose social consciousness, on the average, is well above that of most groups in our society. If there were obvious ways the press could make a greater contribution toward international understanding, journalists themselves would have called attention to them.

Nearly all daily newspapers have established regular mechanisms for self-criticism, according to a study by William B. Blankenburg of the University of Wisconsin. (ANPA News Research Bulletin, 1970.) One of the major themes at the 1970 meeting of the American Society of Newspaper Editors was that inadequate press coverage had contributed to the problems of the United States, domestic and foreign. (Brown, 1970.) Both the Associated Press and United Press International, in addition to maintaining facilities for internal self-criticism, publish newsletters that have as a major purpose the airing of criticisms of their service made internally or by users. (The two publications are AP Log and UPI Reporter. They give credit to their own staffers who turn in exceptionally good performances, which is in itself a form of criticism, but they also highlight errors and mistakes of judgment. The willingness of the wire services, and the news media in general, to engage in rather sharp self-criticism contrasts markedly with their sensitivity to criticism from outside sources, and their apparent resentment of it.) The spate of books sharply criticizing the mass media and written by journalists is unending. (For example, Aronson, 1972; Bagdikian, 1972.) Journalism reviews, designed to give exposure to the weaknesses of the press, have sprung up in at least a dozen cities.

As might be expected in view of these circumstances, a large proportion of the criticisms of the quantity and quality of news coverage, and of the role of the media in our society, originate with media personnel. When one asks how the press might make a greater contribution toward the solution of international problems, one does not pose a brand-new question.

Of course, self-criticism is a matter of degree and there are those who would urge the mass media to go farther. For instance, one press critic, after noting the conclusion of the National Commission on the Causes and Prevention of Violence to the effect that the press was reluctant to undertake self-analysis, added: "[This] is unfortunately true. The press not only is reluctant but fiercely resists self-analysis." (Tebbel, 1970, p. 69.) This statement has important objective referents, as do other similar statements that could be found, but in evaluating it one should not forget that its author is a prominent journalist and was writing in a mass medium—the Saturday Review.

CONSTRAINTS ON THE PRESS

The first step toward making practical suggestions with regard to the role of the commercial press in conflict resolution is to recognize the constraints or limitations under which it operates. One can then either try to think of ways the media could make greater contributions within the limits of these constraints or devise ways the constraints might be loosened or circumvented.

A major constraint is that the press has numerous functions to perform and cannot safely neglect any of them. While it can and does contribute toward peace-keeping and peace-making, and might contribute more, it also helps to satisfy innumerable needs of individuals, including relaxation and entertainment; it provides a counterweight to governmental power; it binds people together into communities; and it helps to assure the continuity of a nation's cultural character. It must attract readers or listeners not only by serving their informational needs but by maintaining a fairly light tone. It must bring news promptly. It cannot afford to be overly repetitious. Any commercial medium that failed to satisfy the expectations of its audience would not survive for long.

As far as increasing the quantity of international news is concerned, the problem is much more with the public than with the press. Relatively few people are willing to spend more than minutes each day informing themselves about what is happening on the international scene. If there were a mass demand for more information from abroad, there would be more information from abroad. As long as the circle of those who demand more international news is small in comparison with the rest of the population, there will be only a few "elite" media that specialize in international news, and even these will ration their space or time carefully.

However, a former foreign correspondent, who was kind enough to read this passage prior to publication, commented as follows:

> But here editors and journalists are not doing their jobs properly. Enormous demand for foreign news cannot be created; but by better writing and editing, and above all by more imaginative assignments and ideas, a greater public can be won. It isn't right for journalists to duck behind the excuse you give them. They should work harder, and if they did, they could increase the demand for their wares and thus the degree of information about international events. I don't blame people for not reading dreary accounts of what diplomatic sources revealed.

A second major constraint is that the resources available to the commercial press for gathering and disseminating news are small when compared with the job to be done. Fewer than one thousand full-time foreign correspondents account for most of the news of other countries published or broadcast in the United States. (Hohenberg, 1969, p. 415.) Some areas of the world are very thinly covered. At any one time, for instance, there are likely to be only a handful of full-time reporters from the United States media in South America, and large parts of Africa and Asia are covered only when a crisis arises. Even so, the media are able to use only a small percentage of the information relayed to them from abroad by their own correspondents and by the wire services, partly because of limitations imposed by newspaper space or broadcast time, partly because of a low level of interest among the mass public.

Third, the definition of news that has grown up in Western society tends to limit what events are covered and how they are covered by the commercial media. Several factors have been identified as contributing to newsworthiness. The larger the number of these factors that can be incorporated in a news report, the more likely it is to be given prominence by the media; the lower the number, the more likely it is to be ignored. Some of these (adapted from Galtung and Ruge, 1965) are as follows:

1. Brevity of time period involved. Events that take minutes, hours, or days are more likely to be reported than events taking weeks, months, or years.

2. Loudness or prominence. A mass meeting at which 50,000 people gather receives greater attention than one attracting 500.

3. Unambiguity. Is it easy to understand what happened?

4. Meaningfulness to the audience. Does it deal with people or places with which they are familiar? Can they identify with someone involved in the event?

5. Consistency with the audience's existing ideas. Does it fit their stereotypes? Is it something they can visualize?

6. Unexpectedness. Is it something that happens rarely, like a total eclipse of the sun? Is it something quite unpredictable?

7. Continuity. Is it something that has already been defined as "news" or part of a big story?

8. Balance. Does it help fill up space or time already allocated for a particular type of story? (On a "dull" day in Washington, there will be reports on national news that on busier days could not find space on the news wires.)

9. Reference to large or powerful nations.

10. Reference to prominent persons.

11. Reference to a "human" dimension, rather than dealing only with inanimate objects.

12. Reference to something negative: dishonest officials, a destructive fire, a war.

Not all these factors are present in every news item that is given prominence, and an item deficient in some of them may make up for this by having a larger component of others. A major sports event may combine nearly all factors quite neatly: It takes place within a reasonable length of time, it is attended by thousands of people, its outcome is unambiguous, people can emphathize with the players, it conforms to the stereotype of what a sports event ought to be, the score is unpredictable, it has already been defined as "news," the media have already assigned space or time for coverage of sports, it may involve teams from large nations, it probably involves well-known persons, and it definitely has a human quality. The only factor usually not included is a reference to something negative, although even this disability may be removed if the fans riot or players are guilty of serious misconduct.

Indeed, it is quite possible that sports make news not because they conform to the definition of what news is but because the working definition of news has been derived in part from sports coverage. Certainly the tendency of reporters to transform international conflict into a grim sporting event is a strong one: There is the box score of men killed or planes shot down, there is the effort to identify winners and losers, there is the attempt to personalize the players, and sometimes even sports terminology is used—such as references to the "team" or to a "foul blow."

Our habituation to sports reporting may distort our understanding of international conflict. A sports event is, in the language of mathematics, a zero-sum game where if one side wins the other side has to lose. In international conflict, both sides may lose, or possibly both may gain something, but there is not necessarily a symmetrical relationship between the gains of one and the losses of another. Sports reporting is unintentionally dishonest in that the focus on the contest obscures the enormous amount of cooperation between the contestants: the acceptance of the referees' authority and the often complicated infrastructure of rules, prior arrangements, and sponsorship. Thus, if we view an international conflict with the eyes of a sports fan, we are likely to fail to recognize some of its most distressing aspects. Finally, the consumer of sports news is primarily a spectator. Unless he has wagered a large sum, he is essentially unaffected by the outcome; even if his team loses and his bankroll declines, he can look forward to future wins. The tendency of the press to make people spectators of international conflict hides from them the possibility that their own fortunes and futures may be involved.

Whether or not sports reporting influences the character of international reporting, the fact that conflict and crisis tend to be emphasized in stories from or about other countries has been well documented. An analysis of several categories of foreign news stories during the 1961-63 period, for instance, found that the stronger the element of conflict, crisis, unpleasantness, or inhumanity in a story, the greater the probability that it would be given space or prominence. (W.L. Gould, 1968.) During the three years covered there were nine front-page stories in the New York Times on cultural exchange between the United States and the Soviet Union. Five of these dealt with the arrest of Yale Professor Frederick Barghoorn by the Soviet police. This incident accounted for 14 of the 26 stories, including those on inside pages, published during 1963. Other students have made very similar observations. (Östgaard, 1965, pp. 48-51.) A conflict or crisis is likely to contain many of the factors that make for newsworthiness, and therefore tends to receive prominence.

At the same time, it is difficult to dramatize the forces or events making for international understanding, conciliation, or cooperation. An international negotiation usually extends over a long period of time, there is secrecy involved, the issues are not clear to the public, often it is not apparent what the "score" is, it is difficult to dramatize. Newsmen make valiant efforts to produce readable copy about negotiations, but they find it difficult since many of the factors making for news are just not present. Only if one delegation walks out, if wild charges are made, or if a crisis in the negotiations develops does reporting become lively.

Coverage of the United Nations offers many of the same problems. A German writer notes that it is easy to complain about the weaknesses of the United Nations, its slowness to act, and its structural deficiencies, while overlooking its vital importance—the fact that it is one of the few forces holding the nations of the world together and is a facility for negotiation that can be used when vitally needed. (Schieder, 1968, p. 890.) To popularize the concept of international law as an instrument for reconciling conflict is even more difficult.

An analysis of several international interactions during the 1960s, prepared for the U.S. Arms Control and Disarmament Agency, found that the arousal of interest in conciliation phases, as measured by space allocation and the location of items on the newspaper page, was slower than in crises. (Walton et al., January 1969, p. 28.) On the other hand, "arousal of interest in response to threats was rapid." But how does one write about conciliation in a way that will convince an editor to use the story when he has so much more "interesting" news at hand? And if he uses it, how many people will read it?

The relative ease with which threats and crises may be turned into news helps to make the press an essential component in an arms race. The process has often been noted. First there are stories, sometimes originating with military spokesmen, that the Soviet Union is overtaking the United States in some branch of weaponry. Then there are stories about worried reactions by congressmen and other leaders. Finally, a money bill is introduced. This process, in turn, stimulates military spokesmen in the Soviet Union, and possibly other countries, to agitate for larger budgets. One side provides a justification for the other to increase its armaments. (Galbraith, 1969; Reston, 1969.)

A former director of the Pentagon's Office of Defense Research and Engineering has given an example of the way the press was used in an effort to gain authorization for the development of a nuclear-powered aircraft. Since some officials could not be convinced that such an airplane would be either feasible or useful, proponents of the project leaked information to the press to the effect that the Soviet Union already was far advanced in developing an aircraft of this nature. There was, in actuality, no evidence that this was the case, and the leaked story failed to keep the project alive. (York, 1970.)

On some occasions it seems as though military spokesmen in one country are actually trying to assist their supposedly unfriendly counterparts in another. Thus, when establishment of an anti-ballistic missile system in the United States was being debated, with its opponents insisting that it would not work, Soviet Marshal Grechko was quoted as saying: (New York Times (February 24, 1970): "We possess weapons capable of reliably hitting enemy aircraft and missiles irrespective of height or speed of their flight, at great distances from the defended targets." Similarly, in August 1969 the Times ran the headline "A Soviet Marshal Sees U.S. Threat" over a story inspired by a Soviet newspaper article, while in September the headline "Admiral

Warns of Soviet Fleet Gains" called attention to an article published in the official journal of the Navy League of the United States. (New York Times, August 31 and September 28, 1969.)

We cannot know how great a role such headlines and stories actually play in an arms race; in some cases their effects may be substantial and in others small. An analysis of the major sources of popular support for more aggressive military initiatives by the United States in the Korean and Vietnam wars found that people who held "tough" attitudes also paid more attention to the mass media, especially newspapers and magazines. (Hamilton, 1968.) Again, it would be presumptuous to say that the media caused these attitudes—other factors were certainly more important—but at least the correlation is suggestive.

If the currently used definition of news does not help to establish a crisis atmosphere, with all the negative results for international comity that this implies, it certainly does not promote a mood more favorable to the conciliation of differences among nations. It also causes resentment in countries that are given little attention by media in other parts of the world except when they suffer some kind of disaster. This may not contribute directly to major conflicts, but it makes cooperation between rich and poor countries more difficult.

A speaker at the Ljubljana Symposium called the definition of news used in the Western press "destructive," observing that the emerging underdeveloped countries were victimized by it. He complained that "calamities, disasters and political troubles are front-page news" but that these countries' efforts to strengthen their economies and their cultural and artistic achievements were ignored. (Mankekar, 1969, p. 235.) Similar remonstrances can be heard at almost any international gathering where representatives of developing countries are present.

Professionals in journalism point out that bad news does not have to dominate, that the mass media do not have to specialize in crisis and disaster to survive. But they also acknowledge that it is easy to feature conflict, crime, and scandal, while it takes work to find news in happy people and peaceful nations. (Hohenberg, 1969, p. 69.) Furthermore, an editor who takes pains to balance the bad news with the good is likely to find that people remember the bad news and forget the rest since bad news makes a stronger impression. In other words, the criteria of news selection for which the media are often castigated are the same criteria that individuals tend to use when they make their own selection from the daily fare available to them.

The process by which information travels from one country to another lowers the quality of communication still further. Just as the individual reporter selects the items he feels conform most closely to his definition of news, editors all along the line of transmission make further selections and relay only a portion of the items they receive. Wire service reports originating in Western Europe, for instance, will be screened by editors in London before being sent to the United States. In New York, editors will screen the news from London and forward to the media only the items they think are most likely to be used. Newspaper and broadcast editors then select from the news file they receive and make available to their audiences the materials they feel are most important or interesting. As a result, only a small percentage of the information sent from any individual country is likely to become available to audiences in another country. (Schramm, 1964, pp. 81-84.)

Even foreign correspondents who report directly to an individual newspaper or broadcast organization often find that their editors back home not only select from what they send in but also may rewrite it. A study of news coverage of the Eighteen-Nation Disarmament Conference in Geneva in 1968 found that some correspondents at the conference felt their editors did violence to the stories they wrote about it. "They stand my copy on its head to make it more exciting," one complained. Others said that their papers would only print stories conforming to editorial policy. However, most believed that their copy was used in much the form they wrote it. (L. N. Gould, 1969, p. 15.)

A frequent complaint of foreign correspondents is that their editors instruct them to cover events that are attention-getting but not very significant, or that they are not allowed to do interpretive reporting that would help to place events in context. A correspondent who had served in Vietnam, for instance, told a member of our research group that in his opinion the American public was essentially ignorant of what was going on in that war-torn country because editors insisted in having "hard news of crises."

Other factors that tend to lower the quality of international communication include the prejudices of individual reporters and editors, government censorship and news management, news transmission costs (it is usually cheaper to send cables from a developed country to a developing one than the other way around), and the political and economic interests of publishers or broadcasters. (Östgaard, 1965, p. 50.)

One effect of these biasing factors is that audiences in different countries have their attention drawn to different events occurring throughout the world, or to different aspects of the same event. A common focus of attention is lacking, thus making two-way communication between nations more difficult. The Swedish Peace Research Institute's study of the Eighteen-Nation Disarmament Conference noted this wide variation in reporting. (Forsberg, 1969.) On a single day, for instance (July 16, 1968), stories about the conference were head-lined as follows in several leading papers around the world:

AFTER THE TREATY TO PREVENT THE SPREAD OF
NUCLEAR WEAPONS (Asahi, Japan)
POWERS WANT SEA WITHOUT BOMBS (O Estado,
Brazil)
TOWARD THE NEXT PHASE (Pravda, Soviet Union)
BRITAIN "NOT ARMED" FOR GERM WARFARE (Daily
Mirror, Great Britain)
BRITISH SEEK TO END ATOM TEST DISPUTE (New
York Times, United States)

The study also found great variations in the space devoted to reports from Geneva in individual newspapers. Thus, during the time period studied, O Estado printed 172 column centimeters on the conference, the New York Times printed 11, and leading newspapers in several countries carried nothing. Papers in countries whose delegates spoke at the conference naturally devoted more attention to these speeches than did papers in other countries. They also tended to give more space to speakers from allied nations. (Forsberg, 1969, pp. 30, 68-70.) Perhaps more significantly, only one paper reported more than half the major proposals made at the conference, and no two papers focused on the same positions or even the same set of subjects for negotiation. Thus readers in different countries were left with different conceptions about the main points at issue and the various positions taken on those points. (Forsberg, 1969, pp. 64, 66.) Under these conditions, it is difficult to see how an international dialogue could develop among those who were not present at the conference and did not have access to some other source of information about what was happening there.

By cumulating factors in the news collection and transmission process that tend to cause bias, it is easy to give an exaggerated picture of the distortions that can result. Furthermore, the example of the Geneva Conference is an extreme case since conferences of this type are among the most difficult to report. Rather than dwelling on the low quality of international communication, perhaps one should emphasize how much information does get through in fairly accurate form, despite the extreme difficulties caused by human and structural factors in the news process.

Nevertheless, it is also clear that there is room for improvement. The media do give the impression that the world is more conflict-laden than it really is; they contribute less than would be desirable to establishing an atmosphere conducive to peaceful settlement of disputes or to facilitating mechanisms for conflict resolution; and

on many subjects they do not provide information on which an international dialogue could be based.

Nor are the mass media very successful in providing early
warning of possibly dangerous situations. Their tendency to emphasize
actual crises makes it difficult for them to devote adequate attention
to potential trouble spots. Correspondents are concentrated in areas
where there is conflict already; other areas are more thinly covered.
Until about 1964, when U.S. military personnel began to be heavily
involved in Vietnam, the American mass media gave only sporadic
attention to Southeast Asia. It was considered an area unworthy of
full-time coverage by most news organizations, although a handful
of reporters were usually on the spot. (Welch, 1972.) Today Korea,
where a major American military force is stationed, is also considered
uninteresting and not a single American correspondent is resident
there. So a vicious cycle develops. Readers do not consider an area
important if it is not covered by press or broadcast news; editors do
not consider it important if there is no indication that their audiences
would be interested. One well-known foreign news editor remarked
in a personal interview, "It is not the duty of the press to take the
public by the hand and lead it."

The tendency of the press to ignore areas not already in the
news was noted by several of the journalists and area experts who
contributed to a survey of foreign news coverage made by the Columbia Graduate School of Journalism in 1963. (Yu, 1963.) One correspondent went so far as to generalize that the greater the information
need, the worse the coverage, "perhaps because people prefer to deal
with the familiar." Experts on Asia, Africa, and Latin America con-
curred, suggesting that not only are there too few correspondents to
cover the globe but that they are unevenly distributed. Another pointed
out that in 1963 the New York Times had 15 correspondents based in
Europe, with its 300 million people, but only six in Asia, with a population of 1.5 billion. Ten years later the number of full-time Times
correspondents in Asia, including the Middle East, had risen to 11.
There were 14 based in Europe, 3 in Africa, and 3 in Latin America.

There are sound economic reasons for this. It costs more than
$40,000 a year to maintain one correspondent at a foreign post, and
the cable and telephone expenses are also substantial. To station a
reporter in a little-known part of the world on the chance that a major
news story might develop there is an expensive gamble; it is a sounder
use of the available resources to station correspondents at points
where the flow of news is likely to be constant. As to the roving correspondent, a news executive told the Columbia survey, that his chances
of being at the right place at the right time are "like playing Russian
roulette." (Yu, 1963.)

"Stringers"—part-time correspondents paid by the line, usually nationals of the countries from which they are reporting—do cover most areas of the world for the major news services and some newspapers. They often provide a kind of trip-wire mechanism. If it looks as though a major story is developing, the stringer reports this and full-time correspondents are rushed to the scene. Many stringers are highly qualified newsmen and their reporting is distinguished. Others, probably a majority, do newswriting only as a sideline and are not equipped to handle difficult subjects. Since they usually are nationals of the countries from which they report, they are also subject to greater pressure from the local government and can be given somewhat less support by their employers. But without stringers the world would be far more ignorant about itself than it is now.

Even when a full-time correspondent or an expert stringer is on the spot, detecting an incipient conflict is not easy. To write it up in a manner that will convince editors to use it in place of some "hard news" item is even more difficult. Early warning involves speculation, considerable explanation of unfamiliar facts, and sometimes complex reasoning. A story of this nature will also take longer to write than a "hard news" story, and the correspondent usually is under great time pressure. This kind of story also requires in-depth knowledge of the country concerned, and preferably knowledge of the local language. (One correspondent remarked in the 1963 survey: "No American newsman has as yet placed South Africa in proper perspective, because none speak Afrikaans.") And if a correspondent spends several days investigating a potentially dangerous situation that has not yet received wide attention, he is likely to be scooped on the front page of his own newspaper by a wire service man who has been following the hot story of the moment. At least under present conditions, it is very difficult for the press to provide early warning of more than a small percentage of the conflicts that arise to plague the world.

INCREASING THE CONTRIBUTIONS OF
THE MASS MEDIA

Given the constraints under which commercial media currently operate, there appear to be four courses of action that might enable them to make a greater contribution to international understanding: One would be to loosen some of these constraints through education of the public; another would be to suggest ways that journalists could help to increase the quantity and quality of international communication while operating within the limits of present constraints; a third would be to experiment with new practices and devices that might be introduced into the system as it now exists; and a fourth would be to provide the commercial media with additional news resources.

Education, the first avenue, is one along which progress is likely to be slow. This is especially true with respect to educating the public with regard to foreign affairs so that more and more people will accept—and demand—more and more information from abroad, and of increasingly high quality. Part of this task is being accomplished through formal educational institutions; part through private bodies concerned with foreign affairs, such as the American Association for the United Nations, the Foreign Policy Association, and the Council on Foreign Relations; and part through the press itself. That is, if the mass media provide more high-quality information from abroad, and find ways to interest people in it, the circle of those demanding such information will increase, thus providing economic justification for more foreign correspondents, more column-inches in the press, and more time on radio and television.

That this public education process is not impossible, even though it takes time, is shown by the steadily expanding circulation of specialized publications that report or discuss foreign affairs.* Another indicator is the growth of university courses and programs specifically related to conflict resolution. As of 1970, about 150 institutions were offering such courses and the number was expanding rapidly. Some 300 college and university courses were using materials provided by the World Law Fund, and almost 2,000 faculty members were receiving the fund's Progress Report. (Washburn, 1971.)

It would be helpful if each peace-related course or program could include a section on the mass media, giving consideration to the kinds of information that are useful in conflict resolution, media practices that tend to exacerbate international tensions, the desirability of providing early warning of situations that might endanger international peace, and so on. Over a period of years these courses would probably be able to increase public demand for more thorough media coverage of foreign affairs.

Commercial mass communication could be influenced more directly through the education of journalists. Journalism education is here used to mean not only study in journalism schools but also the many formal and informal processes through which reporters, editors, and executives at all stages of their careers develop new ideas and explore new possibilities. The three-week seminars for news specialists of many types, conducted by the American Press

---

*For example, between 1949 and 1969 the circulation of the quarterly Foreign Affairs increased from 19,497 to 73,000.

Institute, as well as mid-career programs at several universities, are examples of the kinds of continuing education in which journalists may be involved.

Through these various educational processes it should be possible for many journalists to become aware of the ways that factors currently making for newsworthiness may work against their own goal of providing an accurate picture of the human environment—and not only when it comes to foreign affairs. While no individual journalist or news organization can change these factors—the public must change, too—the definition of news has enough elasticity to allow for various ways of handling a story. (Hohenberg, 1969, pp. 67-70.) In writing about other countries and peoples it is possible for the reporter to search consciously for unifying factors as well as divisive ones.

It is possible to seek out third parties who can comment impartially on a conflict, rather than allowing the contesting parties to dominate the story with the result that their remarks tend to inflame each other. It is possible to reject stereotypes of other nationalities— in fact, it is relatively easy once one is conscious of the stereotype— and the contrast between a prevailing stereotype and reality may contribute to newsworthiness. It is possible to become aware of the danger of the self-fulfilling prophecy—that by predicting an event a reporter may implicate himself in bringing it about. It is possible to appreciate the role of the press in arms races, and to supplement leaked reports that "the other side is overtaking us" with statements from more disinterested observers of military affairs. Rather than making a good story out of each governmental statement (or nongovernmental statement, for that matter) that a crisis exists, the journalist can make an equally good story by blowing the whistle on those who create false emergencies. Indeed, this is part of the watchdog function of the press.

Violence and crises do make news, but is such heavy reporting of violence really necessary even under current conditions? A comparison of Canadian Broadcasting Corporation newscasts with those of a leading American network, conducted during the spring of 1970, showed that the Canadians managed to survive with less than half the violence shown on American television. (B. D. Singer, 1970-71.) And surely the Canadian journalists have no lower professional standards.

As journalists become more aware of the role the press can play in facilitating peaceful solutions—or in making them more difficult— it is to be expected that more will take this factor into account in their own day-to-day work. Just as reputable journalists now weigh the value of public disclosure against the value of protecting national security or protecting an innocent person from harm, and sometimes handle a story differently as a result, they could also weigh news value against the danger of exacerbating international conflict. Indeed, the greatest contribution of journalists to a more peaceful world may come about as a result of the cumulative effect of such individual decisions.

At the same time, journalism education can make those in the profession more widely acquainted with research on ways mass communications can work for or against international understanding. For instance, the investigations of one student strongly suggest that attempts to link various international issues in order to show a pattern or conspiracy, have the effect of promoting a sense of crisis and lowering international trust. This happened in the fall of 1961, when the Berlin and Cuba issues were associated in the press. At the same time, journalists suggested that there was a relationship between American bases in Turkey and Italy and the Cuban missile crisis. Linking the three issues tended to heighten tensions. (L. N. Gould, 1969, pp. 296, 297.) Of course, when there is clear evidence that various issues are associated, the newsman must present this, but he can also be aware of the dangers of speculation.

Another researcher, in a study of editorials in the London press, found that the newspapers did not seem to be aware of the full range of possibilities for the resolution of international conflict. In their comments on international disputes, the newspapers tended to advocate either reconciliation between the parties or the use of force, while overlooking the possibilities of mediation and arbitration. This contrasted with their recommendations with regard to domestic conflict, where mediation and arbitration were suggested much more often. (Coddington, 1965.) Here again, greater awareness of the possibilities on the part of reporters and editors might make a difference in mass media content. Those concerned with journalism education can ensure that research findings such as these—which are likely to increase in number as peace research institutes proliferate—are communicated to the press. Journalists will naturally question these findings and reject some; others may be accepted.

Journalism education has already recognized the importance of background information, of setting events in context and explaining their meaning. This trend is likely to continue. It is generally accepted among journalists that there is less and less "hard news"— news that can stand by itself without interpretation. Thus, one can report that a currency has been devalued. The fact itself is hard news, but what does it mean? The reader must have interpretation or the "hard" news is meaningless. Social scientists can be of service by specifying in greater detail the kinds of interpretation that are necessary to facilitate understanding. One recommendation is that a report about any event should be able to answer two questions: What does it mean to those involved? And what is its significance for the reader, listener, or viewer? (Buchanan and Cantril, 1953.) Another researcher suggests that the goal of communication should be to enable one person to take the other's role, to see the world as the other sees it. Thus it is not enough to know what attitudes are held by another person; it is also necessary to know why he holds them. (Angell, 1969, p. 30.) Much more systematic work on specifications for "in-depth" stories is necessary, and as yet the social scientist can offer the journalist only approximate guidance. But whatever research has been done should be made available.

At the same time that journalism education pursues its deliberate course, the mass media could engage in more vigorous experimentation in searching for ways to present news more completely and more faithfully. How can one build a larger and more attentive audience for international news? How can one deepen understanding among those who are already seriously interested? How can distortion caused by news definitions and the long, tortuous news channels be minimized? Some concrete suggestions have been made, but few of these have been thoroughly investigated.

A possibility that deserves more extensive exploration is that of inviting journalists, and possibly others, from one country to contribute directly to the mass media in another. This would help eliminate at least some of the distortion that takes place in news channels. A newspaper, for instance, could reserve a regular column for foreign contributors. Television news could introduce foreign commentators as a regular feature. Of course, difficulties would be caused by the fact that journalists, like the rest of us, often do not know how to communicate effectively with people from other societies; cultural and semantic difficulties would be experienced. But these difficulties could be minimized by linking guest columnists and commentators with exchange programs. Foreign newsmen could come to the United States to study ways of communicating with American audiences for a year or more before starting to contribute to the American mass media. In some cases, journalists from other countries who had been stationed in the United States for some years as foreign correspondents might already be qualified. American journalists could contribute to foreign media along similar lines.

Another possibility is to experiment with the presentation of news as drama, as has so often been done with history. This approach might be especially suitable for the electronic media. A dramatic presentation allows audiences to identify with people about whom they know little and with whom they may never have personal contact. And there is no reason why the facts presented in dramatic form could not be as accurate as the facts presented by conventional reporting. Footage in a newscast or documentary may portray wars, floods, or famines, but the viewers remain spectators—the people involved are strangers

who dress differently, may belong to a different race, and speak a
different language. But a six-minute mini-play, using actors from
the country concerned, and dubbed in English, would be likely to change
the viewers from spectators into participants. There are tremendous
organizational and economic difficulties involved in this form of news
presentation, but it is unlikely that they are insuperable. Dramatic
forms already have been used to illuminate race relations in the United
States, and the British Broadcasting Corporation devoted three hours
of prime television time in 1970 to a dramatization of the Chicago
conspiracy trial. The result, in the words of the New York Times'
report (October 6, 1970) was "an extraordinary projection of the total
conflict of values played out in the Federal courtroom." There is no
reason why this approach could not be used to explicate international
problems as well. Preparation of such dramatic sequences would
involve close collaboration among newsmen, dramatists, and nationals
of all countries concerned. Once institutionalized, this cooperation
should not be difficult to sustain and apply to numerous situations.

A suggestion for innovation by the mass media that deserves
further exploration has been made by Johan Galtung. He proposes
that an international panel of experts who are prepared to appear on
worldwide television should be established. Whenever an international
crisis appears to be in the offing, the appropriate experts should be
asked to discuss it before a world public, presenting a wide variety
of views. Galtung says, "The important thing here is . . . to have a
sort of idea factory that can function in the open." There are many
think tanks functioning in private, he points out, but an open one might
help to bring about consideration of new alternatives by governments
and to cut through the insulation that often surrounds decision-makers.
Especially in times of impending crisis, such programs would be likely
to attract substantial audiences. (Galtung, 1970, pp. 28-29.)

Fictional materials used by the mass media also play a role in
the advancement of international understanding when they give a
faithful picture of people in other societies, unmarred by stereotypes,
when they contribute to a mood favorable to conflict resolution, and
when they confer prestige on the peace-maker. Some do this already.
For example, a popular "western" television drama "Alias Smith and
Jones" presented a sequence in 1972 that revolved around the efforts
of the two protagonists to make peace between an avaricious Texas
landlord and a fierce Mexican grandee. It cannot be said that this
program avoided stereotypes, but it had the virtue of explaining the
positions of both sides in the dispute and leading the viewer to identify
with the mediators. In a few other popular programs, the "good guy"
has a foreign accent. Systematic exploration of the ways that entertainment content might make a greater contribution to nonviolent conflict resolution would be well worthwhile. Indeed, this might prove

to be television's main line of defense against the accusation that its fictional materials tend to glorify violence.

Consideration should also be given to the contributions that technological innovations might make toward a more peaceful world. Some thought, although not nearly enough, has been given to the role of television satellites in bringing peoples together, but less dramatic developments have received little attention. One promising approach has been pioneered by NHK, the Japanese Broadcasting Corporation, which broadcast television programs on the Expo-70 fair in such a manner that viewers could receive the program in more than one language. "Multiplex television receivers" allowed a choice of audio channels with different language versions. (International Broadcast Institute, autumn 1970.)

The number of lines along which the mass media might experiment is limited only by the imagination. Nevertheless, without outside prodding and assistance, the media are unlikely to conduct very much experimentation. This is partly because, like all large bureaucracies, they are resistant to change, and partly because their resources are limited. Although collectively they spend many millions of dollars each year, their profit margin is not large enough to sponsor very many costly experiments, some of which will not work.

Even more important is the fact that the commercial mass media are not set up to collect all news from its original source. They do this in some cases through investigative reporting, but for the most part they merely select information that is already prepackaged and authenticated in some way and process this information through their news channels. Most reports originate with news releases, formal statements, or press conferences of public or private organizations. For instance, well over half the stories on the 1968 presidential election carried in the American newspaper press during the final four weeks of the campaign were attributed to the candidates themselves. (Graber, 1971.) The press has an extremely important critical and investigative function, but it usually investigates and criticizes after some information has already been made available to it.

Other news comes from experts, who have performed the task of gathering the necessary facts, sifting them, and arriving at conclusions. The reporter approaches a government official, scientist, or some other expert, and obtains from him a summary of what he knows about a particular subject. As Bernard Roshco puts it, "The press usually reports the information nearest at hand and easiest to run through a typewriter." (Roshco, 1970.) Commenting on former Vice President Spiro Agnew's complaint that reporters concentrated on the American presence in Laos and ignored North Vietnamese incursions, Roshco goes on to say that if there had been a North Vietnamese briefing officer in Vientiane, Mr. Agnew would not have had to complain. By and large, the press looks to other organizations, or to experts who are usually supported by large organizations, for its supply of news. If there is no organization or expert to put the news out, it is likely to go unreported.

Thus the commercial mass media are primarily processors of second-hand information. When a major fire or flood occurs, reporters are likely to be on the spot, directly reporting what they can observe. But most of their time is spent otherwise: at the police station talking with police spokesmen; at a government press conference or committee hearing, taking down the words of officials or expert witnesses; or interviewing a leading surgeon who has just performed an unusual operation. Journalists also monitor government publications, some specialized journals, and professional meetings. Foreign correspondents spend a large portion of their time reading the foreign press.

To make such observations is not to denigrate the functions of the press in a democratic society. More than any other institution, it binds the society together, makes it possible for the citizen to evaluate the institutions that are supposed to be serving him, and informs members of the public about developments in other societies that may affect them. But in order to perform its vital functions the press must have an extensive infrastructure.

6

**PRIVATE ORGANIZATIONS
AS PART OF THE
PRESS INFRASTRUCTURE**

Part of the press infrastructure is composed of government handouts and spokesmen, but part also consists of private organizations and experts in all sectors of society. Within most organizations, certain individuals gather information and package it in a form that a reporter can use. Sometimes they authenticate it; that is, their authority provides assurance that the information is likely to be significant, correct, or both. (Roshco, 1968.) When an expert seismologist predicts an earthquake, this is news; but it is news because he has spent years gathering and sifting specialized data and because he makes the prediction in his professional capacity. Similarly, a labor leader's remarks about workers' grievances are news both because of his position and because it is assumed that his organization has gathered extensive information on the subject.

A great deal of news originates with interest groups. Political information is prepackaged and given to the press by political parties and candidates. News about the environment often comes from conservation groups. Publicity about manufactured products frequently originates with the manufacturer or with consumer groups. Many subjects would drop out of the news, or would be given much less attention by the media, if interested individuals and organizations were not continuously making statements, issuing press releases, or arranging newsworthy events.

Another part of the press infrastructure involves the technologists who develop the hardware that is used in information transmission. Some devices are developed with the news media in mind, such as the linotype machine or the television satellite. Others, such as the computer, find important applications in the media, even though these uses may not have occurred to the scientists and technologists who originally devised them. Software, as well as hardware, is sometimes developed by specialists outside of journalism. Photographic techniques, for instance, may be originated by experimental artists and later find application in mass communication. Economists or statisticians may devise analytic and presentational devices that are then adopted by the mass media. It is common to find reference to the gross national product in news stories, and the median is now frequently used by the press (instead of the sometimes misleading arithmetic mean) as a measure of central tendency.

Each subject area with which the mass media deal has a unique infrastructure. News sources differ, and the hardware and software required may vary. Some infrastructures are stronger than others. The press often does a good job of covering local politics since it usually has adequate sources of information and also the means of presenting this information in terms that people can understand. It has more difficulty in covering developing countries, in part because prepackaged information is less available and because techniques have not been found for using words and pictures to convey the full flavor of a very different society.

The infrastructure for mass communications that deal with conflict resolution is rather weak; at least, it could be greatly strengthened. A number of organizations could provide resources that would enable the press to increase the quality and quantity of international coverage, to call attention to dangerous situations as well as to opportunities for cementing good relations, to mobilize those concerned with peace-keeping, to provide information that would assist in conflict resolution, and to promote a public mood favorable to peaceful solutions. Various groups already provide some support to the press in the performance of these functions; the problem is to specify how they might do more.

In the private sector, three types of organizations could be particularly useful: those whose major interest is peace-keeping and conflict resolution; those that make intensive studies of particular areas of the world; and those that conduct research on journalism and communication in general.

GROUPS CONCERNED WITH ADVANCING INTERNATIONAL UNDERSTANDING

Organizations devoted to study and action in connection with peace-keeping and conflict resolution are an important part of the infrastructure needed by the mass media. Some issue frequent news releases; others publish distinguished journals; officials of such organizations are sometimes quoted in the mass media. Nevertheless, these groups provide no sources that combine authoritativeness with

71

frequency and convenience of access. The available materials are diffuse; they come across the news desk like a series of publicity releases from a variety of public relations offices and too often end up in the trash basket. It would be more effective if several such groups could combine their efforts and support a regular specialized research and information service, not unlike Science Service or Religious News Service.

The task of keeping public attention focused on factors that tend to unite peoples rather than to divide them is nobody's job at present. Commercial media will report a Pugwash Conference, a memorandum from a prominent Soviet scientist urging East-West cooperation, or a study by the U.S. Arms Control Agency showing that war industries are less profitable than those devoted to peacetime needs. But they usually report each such item only once; then it fades from public attention. News of this type can be kept alive only if some organization is working to keep it alive: obtaining follow-up statements from prominent figures, digging up more information, looking for similar events—and then preparing news releases and submitting them to the mass media. Not all the releases will be used, but some will be and others may inspire reporters to do some additional digging on their own.

A related function of such a specialized information service could be to monitor technical sources, such as the regular reports on arms transfers published by the U.S. Arms Control Agency, and to provide interpretive comments that could be used by the mass media. The information service could do the same for military budgets. Information on arms transfers and military budgets is fairly easily available from several sources, but it rarely receives wide attention or discussion.

The same organization, or a related one, could monitor ongoing social research, industrial conciliation, and indeed any activity that might produce ideas or techniques applicable to peace-making or peace-keeping. It could "translate" these ideas and techniques into language that would be easily understood and would make the relevance to international understanding as clear as possible, and then could release this material to the mass media.

It could also maintain a continuing scrutiny of the world press, watching for signs of serious tensions, as suggested by Karl Deutsch. (K. W. Deutsch, 1957.) If it were able to subscribe to the major international wire services, it could pick up and publicize items signaling possibly dangerous situations that initially were ignored by the major mass media. The wire services themselves have on occassion complained about non-use of such material. For instance, a UPI survey in the spring of 1956 found that many observers of the Middle East were predicting an Arab-Israeli war in the near future, but that use of this material in U.S. media was "disappointing." (UPI Reporter, April 5, 1956.) Perhaps more could have been done to alert peace-keeping agencies.

At times of international crisis, an information service of this nature would be in a position to seek out those who might offer solutions; to see that all major viewpoints were given expression; and to try to ensure that no available mechanisms for the resolution of the conflict were overlooked.

Finally, one or more such specialized news services might provide internal lines of communication for those actively interested in preventing and conciliating international conflict. Several students of international relations, including Walter Lippmann and Bernard Cohen, have pointed out that the relatively small number of people who are seriously concerned with international affairs required sources of current information to supplement the material now supplied by the mass media. Quarterly or monthly journals cannot do the job. If possible, the service should be on a twice-weekly or day-to-day basis, and in addition to providing news and comment on international events the service should keep its subscribers informed of what those with similar interests are thinking and doing.

To construct even one organization that would be capable of performing these publicity and research tasks at all adequately would be a major endeavor. A daily or twice-weekly news service would be an especially complicated operation to mount. Nevertheless, it is probable that the necessary resources are available in the United States and some other countries. Numerous small and medium-sized organizations already devote a substantial share of their resources to research and publicity in the interests of international understanding. If each were to contribute even a small percentage of its budget to a common undertaking, the venture would not fail for lack of funds. Far greater than the economic problem would be the difficulty of overcoming the particularistic tendencies of many of the groups in question—their commitment to a given philosophy or certain types of solutions and their unwillingness to consider other philosophies and solutions. An organizational platform broad enough to include a major portion of the spectrum of those concerned with international understanding would have to constructed. In some cases, support might be sought in several countries, resulting in the formation of multinational organizations. These would have the advantage of incorporating a larger number of viewpoints internally, so that their work would be less likely to reflect the interests of any single nation.

A more modest proposal would be simply that private organizations concerned with peace-keeping and conflict resolution should think of their function as including the provision of resources for the mass media. To this end, they might give more attention to the requirements of print and electronic journalists. Releases should be timed to contribute to major stories of the day; technical materials should be "translated" into easily understood language; important announcements should be made by important people. These and other rules are well known to public relations practitioners. The significant point is that some organizations may wish to consider whether they might be able to make appreciable contributions to their stated goals by devoting more attention to the mass media.

AREA RESEARCH INSTITUTES

Another type of organization that could do more to strengthen the press infrastructure is the area research institute. It is, theoretically at least, able to supplement the work of the mass media and the international wire services by providing further information about various parts of the world and by supplying the background context in which events could be understood.

There already are area institutes in fairly large numbers, some in the United States and some in other countries, but they leave large portions of the world uncovered or very thinly covered. One survey found, in the United States, 203 organized, graduate-level programs dealing with various world areas as of 1969. (Lambert, 1973.) Another survey identified 2,318 "international programs" at American colleges and universities as of 1970, although many of these were "study abroad" programs or others that did not involve extensive research on current affairs. (Academy for Educational Development, 1972.) Yet at the time Fidel Castro came to power, no American scholar had made contemporary Cuba a major focus of his interest. And as of 1965 neither State Department officials nor newsmen were able to find any American academician who could explain Vietnamese Buddhism to them.

Furthermore, many area specialists in the United States are concerned mainly with the past history, the literature, or the exotic aspects of the areas they are studying. A foreign service officer complained to the writer that when you consult an anthropologist about Latin America, he is likely to be able to tell you a great deal about Indian tribes but very little about the people who influence contemporary political and economic policies. Most institutes are too thinly staffed and concerned with too wide an area to be of great help in providing in-depth understanding of contemporary affairs in a single country.

An exception is provided by several institutes on Soviet affairs, where scholars read Pravda, Izvestia, and numerous other Soviet publications as part of their daily routines, in addition to studying Russian history, the Soviet economy, and related subjects. Indeed, one could make a case that there would have been more serious misunderstanding between the United States and the Soviet Union during the past 25 years if American scholars had not been studying Soviet affairs and Soviet scholars had not been giving equally careful attention to American affairs. This is not to imply that each country had completely adequate knowledge of the other. American specialists on the Soviet Union failed to realize the extent of Soviet postwar disarmament, with the result that a major factor that could have had a dampening effect on the cold war was not taken into consideration. Soviet specialists, for their part, seem to have been overly impressed with the "roll-back" rhetoric in the American presidential campaign of 1952. (Brzezinski, 1972.)

As far as Cuba and Vietnam are concerned, it is abundantly clear that the United States made major miscalculations and that these were due in part to sheer ignorance in both private and governmental sectors.

Government officials cannot make up for the gaps in area expertise at American universities. The practice of shifting foreign service personnel from country to country every few years insures that few real specialists develop, and even those who have repeated assignments in the same area are burdened with administrative tasks and can engage in little serious study. Again, there is a notable exception in the case of the Soviet Union, for which several highly qualified government experts were developed. But because of the poverty and thin staffing of most area institutes at American universities, and because the government has not seriously attempted to make up for this, the United States has denied itself an adequate capability of placing current events in context as far as many areas of the world are concerned.

Most other countries are in an even worse situation when it comes to maintaining competent interpreters of events throughout the world. It is probable that the Soviet Union and Poland are best served in this regard. Through their respective academies of science, both maintain staffs of highly knowledgeable experts who can devote themselves to the study of the past history and contemporary affairs of other societies. They are relatively unencumbered by administrative duties and they do not ordinarily serve on the teaching staffs of universities, although some of them lecture occasionally.

A network of area institutes that, collectively, could give adequate attention to all parts of the world would be an extremely valuable resource for several reasons. They could serve as "homes" for scholars from other countries who wished to make use of their facilities, they could assist in training government and private personnel who were preparing to go overseas, and they could provide advice to officials of government or private organizations that had dealings with other countries. But their main function—at least the one that concerns us here—would be to interpret other peoples and events in other countries to Americans, through scholarly publication, through communication with journalists, and through specialized organizations such as those concerned specifically with conflict resolution.

The desirability of establishing networks of area institutes has been pointed out by a British scholar, Frank Edmead, who outlines their structure and functions in considerable detail. He advocates that the map of the world be divided into regions or countries that could be allocated to different analysts or teams of analysts. Each group would then prepare periodic charts of the situations with which it was concerned. These centers might be located "in different countries, established by different types of institutions, organized in different ways, covering different parts of the field and using different procedures." (Edmead, 1971, pp. 40ff.) Although Edmead sees the proposed centers primarily as an aid to mediators, their value as a resource for the press is obvious. The importance of area institutes in promoting good relations among nations also was emphasized by the Third Japanese-American Assembly in 1972, which welcomed the establishment of the Japan Foundation by the Japanese government and called for a vigorous effort to strengthen Japanese area studies in the United States. (American Assembly, 1972.)

There are strong arguments that area institutes should be extra-governmental and that their work should be available to the press and the public. If organized in this way, they could serve as a supplement and a balance to governmental area specialists, who otherwise might have a monopoly of whatever expertise there was on a given area or situation. The danger of concentrating expertise solely within the government—or indeed in any one location—is noted inferentially by Susan Welch, who observes that during the early 1950s the American press obtained most of its information about Southeast Asia from government sources and thus was of limited use in suggesting alternative policies: "The press, by itself accepting basic Administration assumptions, enhanced the probability that others within the political system would also view the situation in the same light." (Welch, 1972, p. 23.)

To establish adequate area institutes in the United States is only part of the problem. Similar institutes to study both the United States and other countries are needed in other nations. For, as far as mutual understanding is concerned, it makes little sense for country A to study country B unless B also studies A. Strong beginnings have been made throughout Europe and in Japan, but less affluent countries will need help. The United States Information Agency has for quite a few years encouraged and partially supported the establishment of "American studies" at foreign universities, but greater efforts are necessary. The United Nations, especially through UNESCO, could play an even more significant role if its financial resources permitted.

The mass media will never be able to make their maximum countribution to the attainment of a more peaceful world unless they are in a position, directly or indirectly, to tap the knowledge of long-time area specialists. We cannot expect the few hundred full-time correspondents, meeting almost daily deadlines, to do the job by themselves.

COMMUNICATION RESEARCHERS

Communication researchers serve as part of the mass media infrastructure in several ways. Through their studies of audiences and information content, they are able to determine which messages are receiving attention and are understood; and sometimes they can suggest new ways of expressing ideas. By studying the institutions that produce media content, they can help identify sources of bias and may be able to encourage corrective action. In some cases they can describe the effects of communications on individuals and social groups and can recommend ways of controlling these effects.

The aspect of communication research with which we are most directly concerned here is its ability to serve as a bridge between the mass media and social research in general. Much of the work done by sociologists, psychologists, and others has implications for the mass media, but these implications must be ferreted out and reformulated before they have relevance for media structure or content. As far as the role of mass communication in the advancement of international understanding is concerned, communication researchers should give particular attention to the work of other social scientists on conflict resolution.

One avenue of research and experimentation that appears promising would be to explore ways in which techniques that have proved useful in advancing understanding among members of small groups could be applied by the mass media to larger publics. For instance, scholars in several countries, notably Leonard W. Doob of Yale University and John W. Burton of the Centre for the Analysis of Conflict in London, have obtained encouraging results by forming small groups of leading citizens from countries in conflict with each other and helping these groups to arrive at a consensus about ways that peace might be restored. (Kelman, 1972.)

Both experimenters operate on the principle that, if the leading citizens chosen to participate in their small group sessions can find a peaceful solution that is satisfactory to all concerned, then there is at least a chance that each participant will be able to persuade political leaders in his own country that such a solution is practicable.

Doob assembled a group of prominent citizens from Kenya, Somalia, and Ethiopia to discuss what might be done about settling the territorial dispute in the Horn of Africa, which has caused strife for many years. Each participant had the explicit or tacit approval

of his government, although none attended as a government representative. The group assembled in an isolated hotel in the mountains of
Italy, and during the first week participated in sensitivity training
to develop communication skills. "T-groups" were formed and they
discussed such issues as the nature of conflict, student unrest, and
the Organization of African Unity. They also played games, engaged
in exercises common to many T-groups, and conducted simulations—
for example, a disarmament game. Then, during the second week,
the participants struggled to come up with a solution to the problem
of the Horn of Africa that would satisfy everyone. Perfect agreement
was not achieved, but there were significant limited agreements, new
approaches to a solution were explored, and most participants came
to appreciate that their "opponents" were reasonable men of good will.
(Doob et al., 1969, pp. 249-66.)

Burton conducted several somewhat similar small group discussions, involving participants from quite a few nations, but he does
not tell us which nations these were. His technique differed in that
he did not make use of formal sensitivity training but instead introduced a number of neutral "third parties" into the discussion. The
role of these third parties was to suggest new ideas, to introduce
historical parallels, and to intervene in order to prevent head-on
collisions. The third parties were not experts on the problems being
discussed, but they were social scientists who had studied conflict
resolution. By speaking from real or simulated ignorance of the
details of the conflict, they were able to secure consideration of
alternatives that otherwise might not have received a hearing. Again,
some significant agreements were achieved. Burton summarizes his
technique as follows: "Controlled communication is a means by which
competing values are brought to attention, and alternative goals and
alternative means of achieving goals are discussed." (Burton, 1969,
p. 205.)

The discussions of both Burton and Doob were conducted in
strict privacy; no man was to be held accountable for the opinions he
expressed at the meetings. The problem is how the benefits of such
private discussions in small groups can be extended to larger numbers
of people through the use of the mass media. Would the ideas expressed lose their value if the identities of the participants were
kept secret? Could an actual discussion take place and then be presented in a synoptic film, using professional actors? How can a
sense of real involvement be communicated to the audience? Questions like these have never been investigated.

Numerous other possible applications of social science research
to the mass media remain to be explored. It has been found that the
mere presence of a neutral third party at a confrontation between two
individual opponents facilitates reconciliation or agreement. (Walton,

1968.) Can the mass media somehow serve as such a third party in disputes among nations? Is there any way that "role reversal" experiments, in which each party to a conflict attempts to take the other's point of view, can be adapted to international communication? (Murray and Deutsch, 1968.) Can relatively large publics benefit from exercises developed by social psychologists, such as the "prisoner's dilemma" game? (Rapoport, 1960 and 1967.) (In the "prisoner's dilemma" game, the participants are rewarded if they trust each other and penalized if they do not.) Practical answers to these questions will not be obtained until researchers engage in extensive experimentation and produce pilot films and articles.

A cousin of the games developed by social psychologists is the political game. This form of inquiry, originated by the RAND Corporation, involves the use of groups of foreign policy experts who attempt to simulate future interaction among nations. (Goldhamer and Speier, 1959.) As many as fifty or as few as a dozen persons may be involved. Some play the roles of foreign ministers, some of chiefs of state, some of military leaders, and so on. The objective is for each person, and each group that represents a national government, to anticipate the probable action of actual political leaders and nations and thus to play out future history as realistically as possible. Different assumptions or starting points for the game may be used, and possible courses of action for each nation under these varying conditions can be compared. For the game to be most realistic, each player should be a true expert on his role. A life-long student of French foreign policy may take the part of the French foreign minister, and military men may make military decisions. Sometimes nationals from various countries play the roles of their own political leaders.

The political game has not proved notably successful in predicting major political events. The actual course of history may turn out to have an uncanny similarity to the events in the game, but one cannot count on it. One experimenter simulated international disarmament negotiations and then systematically compared these with the disarmament negotiations of the 1950s. He found that his game did in fact replicate such factors as insecurity, propaganda, and hostility, as well as the timing and type of concessions that were actually made in the historical situation, although the substance of concessions made was different. (Bonham, 1971.) A game on the Middle East, organized by the writer at the Massachusetts Institute of Technology in 1957, predicted the subsequent revolution in Iraq, and a slightly later game fairly accurately forecast developments in Algeria. Nevertheless one could list many more instances in which games and history were in disagreement.

But the game does succeed in uncovering possible courses of action that might not already have been considered, and it clarifies the probable consequences of various alternatives. In addition, it can involve players and spectators very deeply, both intellectually and emotionally. The problems of other countries become real, and one can no longer avoid facing up to difficult or dangerous situations. The game is an intense experience.

If the essence of political games revolving around current international problems could be captured in reasonable length and presented by the mass media, this might well make a significant contribution to international understanding. It would inject into the stream of discussion among elites and attentive publics a number of possible courses of action that might not have been considered. Like the news drama, it would help to demolish stereotypes about other nations and to bring the concerns of other peoples much closer. It might provide an element of early warning, and certainly would call attention to some potentially dangerous situations. It would also provide a dramatic presentation that could deeply involve a large proportion of the elites and attentive publics, and attract new audiences.

To capsule a political game (which may take several weeks to play) in a television program, or in a newspaper or magazine article of reasonable length, will not be easy. Experimentation will be necessary. Nevertheless, journalists and communication technicians have overcome problems at least as difficult in the past, and the game is worth the candle.

Another possible application of these techniques to the mass media would be to incorporate working journalists in political games and problem-solving T-groups. If they gained new insights on international conflicts, and if these insights were reflected in their reporting, they might exercise a more permanent influence than government officials, who may be transferred to other duties or defeated at the polls.

Commercial media will be more likely to invest in publication or broadcasting of materials based on political games or other problem-solving devices if the utility and feasibility of presenting these materials to a mass audience has already been demonstrated. This is a task for researchers and experimenters.

Since all research involves exploration of the unknown, it is difficult to anticipate the ways in which study of the communication process and application of findings from other areas of social research may be able to strengthen the capabilities of the mass media for conflict resolution. Adaptation of small group techniques to large audiences is only one of many possibilities. Development of something that might be called international journalism is another.

International banking, international law, and several other international specialties are well established, but techniques of intercultural communication are still rudimentary. Investigations in this area are particularly pressing in view of the development of new communication technologies. And the question should also be asked in the reverse order. That is, instead of inquiring how new technologies could be used, one might ask: What technologies are required to provide for increased quality and quantity of international communication?

If communication researchers keep in mind their role as part of the mass media infrastructure, and constantly review the implications of their work for conflict resolution, numerous other opportunities for fruitful inquiry will become apparent.

Private organizations devoted to international understanding, area research institutes, and communication research groups are not ordinarily self-sustaining. While they provide part of the press infrastructure, they cannot expect very much support from the press, which is accustomed to receiving information gratis. Area institutes and communication research groups sometimes are partially supported by government agencies. It is to be hoped that this support will continue and increase, but that it will be matched by private funds. Indeed, all three types of organization must rely heavily on foundation grants and individual donations.

If the thesis is correct that mass communication can contribute significantly to a more peaceful world, and if the commercial media require the kind of infrastructure described here to do their part effectively, then it would seem that the private organizations making up the infrastructure deserve generous support.

7

THE U.S. GOVERNMENT
AS COMMUNICATOR

Each national government differs in its capacity to participate in and influence the international dialogue. Some governments have weak voices and control few communication channels; others can easily make themselves heard and have many channels at their command. In general, governments of democracies control only a small part of the communication spectrum in their own countries, while authoritarian or totalitarian governments control or actually operate a much larger share. The U.S. government resembles, in many ways, a private organization that is temporarily designated to administer certain aspects of national life. It has great power due to its prestige and the enormous resources it can allocate, but its sphere of authority is severely limited. One of the bizarre political traits of Americans is to insist that governmental powers be circumscribed while simultaneously complaining that government does not immediately solve all outstanding problems.

In no area are the limitations on the U.S. government more apparent than with respect to communication. Federal authorities directly control a very small part of the communication spectrum. Only a tiny fraction of messages reaching the domestic audience flow entirely through official channels. These messages include those contained in government publications, such as Department of Agriculture bulletins, and in speeches given by federal officials. Communications reaching foreign audiences through U.S. government channels likewise comprise only a small percentage of total messages from the United States. While the United States Information Agency (USIA) operates one of the largest information enterprises in the world, foreign peoples obtain the bulk of their information about the United States from their own domestic newspapers, magazines, and broadcast enterprises, which in turn are likely to be served by one or more international wire services. Some information comes directly from U.S.-produced films, magazines, or books, but most of these are prepared by private bodies in the United States. In a few nations, particularly developing countries, information from or about the United States received through U.S. government channels may amount to as much as a quarter or a third of the total; in others the proportion is far lower. And when one considers the totality of messages about all subjects received by a foreign audience, the proportion arriving through U.S. government channels is miniscule indeed.

The limited communication activities in which the U.S. government engages must conform to certain rules. They must not compete with private enterprise. They must be sanctioned, or at least tolerated, by a majority in Congress. If they appear to be propagandizing the American electorate, or if they depart from American standards of appropriateness or good taste, they are likely to be severely criticized and subjected to political retribution. The shortwave broadcaster speaking over the Voice of America to a distant audience in another country must constantly look over his shoulder to detect reactions from the American press and Congress.

Despite these constraints, the power of the U.S. government to influence communication between the United States and other countries is enormous. This is largely because of its ability to obtain attention in media that it does not control. When the president or the secretary of state speaks, some of what is said will be carried through non-governmental channels to large audiences at home and abroad. Leading officials thus have the power to determine, in part, what is in the news and what will be discussed. (Reston, 1949.) Not only their words but also their actions have the effect of communicating ideas and impressions. (Jervis, 1970.) Whether the device used is a press conference or a presidential visit to another capital, wide attention is assured.

Also important is the government's ability to provide the infrastructure of news: to assemble and release, or to withhold, facts and conclusions. The collection and analysis of many varieties of social, economic, and political data requires enormous resources and a large organization. Often the government is the only body with the necessary capability. Its reports and releases, even though they may cover only part of the data gathered, become a subject for news stories and discussions. Even simpler items, to find their way into the press, must ordinarily be researched and prepackaged by someone—and this someone is frequently to be found in the government bureaucracy. Almost all news requires some minimal level of organization before it reaches the press. (Roscho, 1970.) The huge governmental public affairs and press information staff, drawing on the resources of the bureaucracy, provide a large proportion of this organization.

Nor should the potentialities of the relatively few information channels that are directly controlled by the government be minimized. While their capacity is small, as compared with the capacity of all information channels, they have several compensating strengths. They can be trained with precision on a single audience or a single subject, thus exercising relatively great influence in a narrow sphere. They can sometimes achieve a multiplier effect, as when a government-produced pamphlet is passed from hand to hand and quoted by other media. And they can on occasion set standards of disclosure or coverage: for instance, by distributing complete texts of official documents, the United States Information Agency has helped to reduce biased interpretations based on partial texts or quotations taken out of context.

Through its political and financial power, the U.S. government can help shape both the structure and the use of some communication channels. For instance, along with other governments, it is represented at discussions of frequency allocations for broadcasting and of the utilization of communication satellites. It participates in the United Nations and in various specialized U.N. agencies such as UNESCO. The degree of support it provides to the communication activities of these agencies influences their strength and direction. Government research funds have made possible a number of research studies bearing on the use of communication to advance international understanding, as well as more general studies of the potentialities and effects of communication in general. There is no way to demonstrate whether such studies have in fact influenced either the structure or the content of international discourse, but one can at least recognize that some of them have formulated concepts that open new possibilities.

The extent to which the U.S. government, or any government, can use the resources available to it to build a more peaceful world is limited by other responsibilities. A government may designate the promotion of international understanding as one of its goals, but in addition it is expected to ensure the security and prosperity of its citizens, to nurture the national prestige and culture, and to pursue a variety of other goals. In addition, a government is usually under strong, self-generated pressure to stay in power, and all of its actions are subject to measurement against the criterion of whether they will increase or decrease the likelihood of winning the next election. Therefore the task of securing peace cannot be left entirely to governments; not only are their resources limited but they are subjected to too many conflicting demands.

It is in part because of the multiple functions of government that proposals for the establishment of a Department of Peace in the U.S. government have limited utility. Either such an agency would constitute an empty symbol, soon subject to ridicule as a do-nothing organization, or else it would become a victim of political infighting with government departments serving a variety of needs. Most actions it could recommend would have to be taken through the instrumentalities of other agencies: the departments of State, Defense, and Commerce, the USIA, and many others. It would therefore be faced with an array of competing and often hostile bureaucratic vested interests.

For the U.S. government, or any government, to utilize its powers and resources so as to make a maximum contribution to world peace, it is necessary that each governmental unit be constituted and guided in such a way as to play a constructive role. This task might be accomplished in part by a White House staff with strong executive backing. Even more necessary is continuing public pressure for a series of specific measures affecting individual agencies. The following are a number of steps that might be taken by the U.S. government in respect to international communication.

GOVERNMENT ACTION TO ACHIEVE
COMMUNICATION GOALS

Through its own channels, and through its influence on communications passing through other channels, the U.S. government could assist in the achievement of the goals identified in Chapter 5: increasing the quantity and quality of international communication, providing early warning of dangerous situations, using communication to facilitate adoption of peaceful solutions, creating a mood in which these solutions are more likely to be accepted, and establishing contacts among those actively interested in promoting international understanding.

The greatest single contribution the U.S. government could make toward increasing the quantity of international communication would be to declassify and make available to the press and to scholars much more of the raw information on which its foreign policy is based. This information—from diplomats, intelligence agents, foreign embassies, and other sources—streams into Washington daily in large quantities. At present, most of it is marked "secret" or "confidential," or is simply allowed to repose in file cabinets, and never comes to public attention. Some of it probably should be withheld to protect sources or to avoid giving further currency to manifestly erroneous reports, but the burden of justification should be shifted from those who seek to release information to those who seek to withhold it.

As a matter of routine, the U.S. government publishes a continuous flow of economic data, from both foreign and domestic sources. This is analyzed by scholars, as well as by officials of various agencies, and some of it finds its way into specialized publications or the general press. The same routine should be observed with respect to information bearing on foreign policy. Since there has never been a tradition for releasing such information in any country, ingenuity would have to be exercised in order to find the most suitable forms and procedures. One probably would not want to publish a diplomatic telegram recounting what a foreign office official of country X whispered to the first secretary of the U.S. embassy at a cocktail party, but the digest of public remarks by the foreign minister of that country would certainly be in order. As a very junior government official, prior to World War II, the author recalls a number of descriptions of conditions in Nazi Germany passing across his desk. These had been gleaned by government agents from travelers and refugees and could have provided a valuable supplement to press reports. Yet all of them were classified. The same condition prevailed during the Korean and Vietnam wars: volumes of raw information that would have helped publics in many countries to understand the problems facing government policy-makers remained unavailable to scholars and the press merely because it was collected under governmental auspices.

Governmental resistance to releasing raw political intelligence will be intense. Many reasons why it would be dangerous or expensive or impractical will be adduced. Most of these reasons have been rehearsed many times: Why should a government surrender a potential advantage by letting another government know what information is available to it? Why should a government release information that may later prove to be unreliable, thereby possibly undermining its own credibility? Is it not likely that mistakes will be made and that information received in confidence may be revealed, thereby making friendly sources apprehensive of speaking frankly to U.S. diplomats? What would prevent a government from releasing only information that supports its own policies, thereby turning the process into an exercise in propaganda?

All these objections, and others that could be advanced, have some merit. But the most important consideration is that arguments in favor of a policy of maximum disclosure have hitherto received very little consideration; they have never been systematically weighed against the disadvantages. For instance, publication of raw intelligence would help to reduce uncertainty in international relations since other governments would be able to assess more accurately whether a true or a distorted picture of conditions in their countries was reaching foreign observers. Since uncertainty is in itself recognized as one of the major destabilizing factors in international relations, any reduction in this area would yield substantial benefits. Fuller disclosure would make it more difficult for governments to hide behind the assertion that their policies were based on secret information not available to their critics, thereby encouraging more careful analysis and consideration before policies were adopted. If it should become obvious that information released by a government contained substantial gaps, scholars and journalists would be motivated to close these gaps, thus ensuring that their government received a more accurate picture.

The U.S. government, in particular, would benefit from a policy of full disclosure since it is, in any case, less able to keep secrets than the government of any other major power. (Davison, 1966 and 1966-67.) Rather than being subjected to continuous embarrassment as a result of revelations made by enterprising newsmen or disgruntled employees, it would be protected by the fact that information supporting as well as conflicting with its policies had been made available in advance of controversy. (It should be emphasized, once again, that we are speaking only of factual information. A policy recommendation prepared by an ambassador for the eyes of the president or the secretary of state would have to be treated as a private communication, at least until decisions had been made on the problems with which it dealt. Governments, like other organizations, must be assured that officials can communicate with each other in confidence; otherwise, their functioning will be impaired. Of course there will be borderline cases in which it is debatable whether a given communication should or should not be privileged, and machinery will be necessary to deal with those cases.)

Full disclosure by the United States would exert powerful pressure on other governments to do likewise, much as Soviet publication of diplomatic documents relating to the outbreak of World War I induced other countries to rush their own diplomatic archives into print. A freer and franker international climate would result.

A somewhat similar idea was presented by Edward Teller in a letter to the New York Times, April 4, 1970. Dr. Teller stated that, as an open society, the United States does not perform well in secret enterprises, and that by abandoning secrecy in research it could make faster scientific progress and at the same time demonstrate the advantage of open procedures.

In short, the advantages of full disclosure would seem to outweigh the disadvantages by a wide margin, even for the governments involved, although the primary beneficiaries would be the private citizens of all countries, who bear the main burden of conflict when it arises.

Maximum advantages of governmental disclosure will not be achieved without additional development of what we have called the news infrastructure. If the government were to release large quantities of raw information on international affairs each week, this would overwhelm the facilities of the news industry. A few nuggets might be extracted, but it is doubtful that very many of these could be put into perspective. Most of the material would remain unanalyzed and unreported.

The task of sifting and ordering this large quantity of information would fall mainly on academic centers for the study of foreign areas and on specialized services such as the research staffs maintained by private bodies concerned with the advancement of international understanding. Analyses prepared by academic and other specialists would probably be published in the first instance in journals directed at persons with a serious interest in international affairs. Some of them would then be picked up and given wider circulation by the general press.

It is clear that at the present time academic area institutes and other specialized organizations are too weak to assume this additional burden. They would have to be greatly strengthened by an infusion of new money and personnel.

A second way that governments, and particularly the U.S. government, could augment the quantity of international informational exchange is by devoting much more effort to encouraging two-way communication. At the present time, information tends to flow <u>from</u> industrialized nations <u>to</u> the less industrialized areas of the world, and <u>from</u> the more powerful <u>to</u> the less powerful states. In particular, educated people in other countries tend to know much more about the United States than educated Americans know about the rest of the world. This imbalance provides a fertile breeding ground for both resentment and misunderstanding. It will not be simple to correct since it is based in part on the fact that people in poorer and technologically less advanced countries want and need more information from their more fortunate neighbors than their richer neighbors require from them. Similarly, smaller and less powerful states tend to want more information about larger and more powerful countries than the latter want about the former. Nevertheless, governments could take a number of steps to secure a more equitable balance.

One major move would be for all governments that maintain a foreign information program to earmark a portion of the program's budget for the encouragement of two-way communication. For example, most states now operate shortwave broadcasting services that are used in support of the commercial or foreign policy aims of the sponsoring government. (Davison, forthcoming.) In countries where the government also has domestic broadcasting outlets—and this is true in most of the world—it would be feasible to invite foreign governments to use a portion of broadcast time to explain their aims to the local audience. In countries, such as the United States, where the government is not permitted to operate domestic broadcast facilities for general audiences, program exchanges would have to be arranged on a more indirect basis: Public and commercial broadcasters could be encouraged to extend their facilities to foreign programmers more frequently, American assistance could be offered to foreign short-wave stations preparing programs for American consumption, and overseas facilities of the United States Information Agency could be offered to public and commercial broadcasters who wished to create programs about foreign areas to be aired in the United States.

Similar arrangements could be made with respect to other media. The USIA now assists foreign publishers in locating and translating books about the United States for dissemination abroad. It could do the same for U.S. book and magazine publishers, helping them to secure titles and articles from other countries for publication in the United States. Whether newspapers and magazines would be willing to accept assistance in the location and translation of materials is debatable, but the possibilities should be examined. The motion picture film market is already organized in such a way that a vigorous international exchange exists, but even here it is likely that some of the less affluent countries could be assisted in making more of their cultural heritage available to foreign audiences.

However it is done, the importance of encouraging two-way communication can scarcely be overestimated. Mutual trust is enhanced when all the parties concerned are assured that they are being listened to. (Whyte, 1952.) One-way communication is likely to lead to suspicion or resentment.

The capacity of the U.S. government to increase the quantity of international communication, at least through its own channels, has declined steadily during the past decade. In 1962 the USIA had a staff of approximately 12,000; by 1971 it was about 9,900. While appropriations for the USIA have risen slightly in dollar terms, its budget has declined in terms of purchasing power. Stated in constant 1954 dollars, the USIA's budget amounted to $117 million in 1962 and $92 million in 1971. (H. Loomis, 1971.) Funds for exchange programs were cut even more sharply during the decade. The Fulbright exchange program, under which academic personnel from the United States are sent abroad and foreign scholars come to the United States, was budgeted at $56 million in 1963 but was down to $34 million by 1970. (New York Times, February 15, 1970) The Peace Corps has experienced a comparable decline in funding during the past few years. Shrinkage of government funds has imperiled a number of private institutions engaged in international education. For instance, the Center of Advanced International Studies, maintained in Bologna, Italy, by the Johns Hopkins University since the mid-1950s, found itself in financial trouble by 1970, largely as a result of cuts in State Department support.

Although the amount of public money available for international communication is less important than how it is spent, budget cuts clearly reduce the capability of the U.S. government to increase the flow of information throughout the world. More dollars devoted to this purpose would not automatically bring about a more peaceful world, but whenever it can be shown that additional funds for international communication are likely to contribute to greater understanding, these funds should be made available. The United States Advisory Commission on Information has found it "indicative of the disordered priorities of our time" that 95 percent of our foreign affairs budget is spent for "national defense" while only 5 percent is devoted to diplomacy, communication, and related activities designed to avoid the resort to force. (United States Advisory Commission on Information, 1969.)

The U.S. government should also increase its support for the information activities of the United Nations and its specialized agencies. In 1965 two scholars noted that Congress was tiring of the idea that the United States has to contribute the bulk of financial support for U.N. projects, and signs of heightened fatigue have been apparent since. (Taylor and Cashman, 1965.) It is true that the United Nations cannot be expected to advance U.S. government policies, and this is often mentioned as a reason for lack of official enthusiasm for the world organization, but it is also the reason why communications through U.N. channels are likely to be regarded with less suspicion than those received through governmental channels. The United States has more to lose through the breakdown of world order than any other nation and should cheerfully grasp any opportunity to strengthen communication mechanisms that help bind the nations of the world together.

Governments can likewise help to raise the quality of international communication; they can assist in ensuring that meaning is transmitted from people to people more accurately. They can do this in part by maintaining high standards of honesty and accuracy in their own informational output; in part by working toward international agreements governing communication standards; and in part by conducting or supporting research in intercultural communication.

Honesty and accuracy in governmental communications to foreign audiences have probably been increasing gradually during the past decades. This is not necessarily due to higher standards of political morality but to the realization that in the long run truthfulness is the best propaganda. Falsehood or misrepresentation may lead to short-term advantage, but this is more than overbalanced by a loss of credibility. The decision of the British Broadcasting Corporation at the beginning of World War II that British losses should be reported fully and factually was a major turning point. The British policy worked;

the BBC came to enjoy a reputation for such reliability that even military opponents accorded it a large measure of trust. American and other Allied propagandists, taking their cue from the British, also emphasized frankness and eschewed polemics. This trend did not extend to the Soviets, who continued to engage in large-scale withholding of information combined with vigorous polemics, but at the same time it was rare for Soviet propaganda to make use of untruthful material. Even the Nazis followed the principle of never attempting to deceive their domestic audience about matters they considered vital, although they might try to mislead foreign publics. (George, 1959, p. 143.)

Following the war, the emphasis on honesty continued, at least in propaganda of the Western powers. (White, 1952-53.) Experienced newsmen who have had occasion to listen to Voice of America broadcasts, for instance, have commented favorably on their coverage, balance, and accuracy. In many parts of the world the BBC is still regarded as even more objective.

Honesty and candor are, or course, relative matters, and the degree to which they are thought to be realized varies with the standards and values of the beholder. No communication is likely to be adjudged completely candid by everyone. The analysis by Ralph K. White (1952-53), for instance, advocates greater efforts to achieve objectivity, even though it recognizes that American propaganda already aims at this. The goals of honesty and accuracy must be constantly striven for, although they will never be fully attained.

Nor is a government's credibility judged on the basis of its external propaganda alone. When two government officials make divergent statements regarding a particular policy, when an official agency is shown to have covered up information that should have been made public, or when a governmental spokesman makes a promise that is not carried out or a forecast that proves inaccurate, credibility suffers. The high standards for official information that critics of the American government demand are in themselves a backhanded tribute to the relatively high standards that already exist. It is implicitly accepted that dishonesty is the exception rather than the norm; otherwise, the exceptions would not be noticeable and could not be highlighted as news. Disclosures in 1972 and 1973 that government officials had lied about military operations in Southeast Asia and about the Watergate scandal were sensational in part because they showed such a wide departure from accepted standards.

Complete credibility at home and abroad, like complete candor, will never be achieved by any government. Nevertheless, the important consideration is that a government make strenuous efforts in this direction, and that such efforts be recognized for what they are. A rather unusual example of what may be accomplished by an

official who sets rigorously high standards for himself is provided by
the press representative attached to the U.S. delegation at the Eighteen-Nation Disarmament Conference that met in Geneva in 1968.
Many delegations brought press officers with them, but as the negotiations dragged on all of these except the American spokesman departed.
But he came to be so widely respected that all the journalists at the
conference came to his briefings. Other delegations often sought his
advice about press relations and frequently asked him to mention their
activities to media representatives. In short, he was trusted by all
at the conference, both delegates and newsmen. One East European
reporter told a researcher, "His job is to advance the American point
of view, but lie? No." (L. N. Gould, 1969, pp. 10-12.)
. In a democracy, at least, standards for international communication can be no higher than those observed at home. Indeed, in an open
society it is difficult to draw a line between domestic and international
communications. The complex relationship between trust in one's
own government and trust in foreign governments is illustrated by
one of the conclusions of a study of international assurance:

> Perhaps the most important findings of the case studies
> is that it matters less whether Americans trust the Soviet
> Union than whether they trust their own government when
> it says that Americans either can or cannot trust the
> Soviet Union . . . . [Walton et al., 1969, p. 14.]

A government's words can scarcely be credited abroad if they are
not credited at home. A government can contribute to improved quality
of international communication only if it is able to increase the accuracy and honesty of its communications at home. False reports
emanating from Washington about bombing in Cambodia, or about any
other international subject, undermine international as well as domestic trust.
While the importance of preserving as high a degree of candor
as possible in governmental communications is widely recognized,
it is surprising that no government has an official or agency responsible for this. In the United States there are numerous built-in devices
for ensuring that public moneys are spent and accounted for in accordance with the law. Some irregularities persist, but they are small
in comparison with the diversions of funds that could be expected in
the absence of these devices for ensuring accountability. Yet in the
field of information there is little pressure from inside the government to assure the fullest possible disclosure and to make certain
that this is candid and meaningful. Some office akin to that of an in-
spector-general for information would appear to be desirable. It may
be that this office, following the precedent of the General Accounting

Office, should be responsible to the Congress rather than to the executive. But however the function is administered, its goal should be to increase the quality (in the sense used here) of government communications.

Another way governments can help to increase the quality of international communication is by working toward international agreements governing information standards. Some beginnings have been made, although no attempt thus far has been notably successful. The United Nations Charter condemns "incitement to war and psychological preparation for war by means of propaganda." In November 1947 the U.N. General Assembly unanimously adopted Resolution 110/II, condemning all forms of propaganda that threaten peace; this resolution was confirmed by the General Assembly again in November 1950, but no agreement defining such propaganda was ever reached. (Osolnik, 1969, pp. 9-10.) The right to be informed was included in the United Nations Declaration of Human Rights, but each subscribing government was left to decide for itself what this meant. In 1962 U.S. and Soviet delegations discussing arms control in Geneva negotiated a "Declaration Against War Propaganda," based on a Soviet proposal, but this was later rejected by the Soviet representatives following new instructions from Moscow. (Dean, 1966.) Slightly more progress was made by UNESCO, which in November 1966 adopted a Declaration of the Principles of International Cultural Cooperation that affirmed, among other things, that "every effort should be made in presenting and disseminating information to ensure its authenticity." (Lewis, 1970.) Various conventions on freedom of information have been discussed but never completed. International conversations about satellite broadcasting have dwelled on types of materials that might be prohibited, but few positive standards have been suggested. The 35-nation Helsinki Conference on European Security and Cooperation in the summer of 1973 spent considerable time discussing restrictions on the free exchange of persons and ideas across Europe, but the extent to which a meeting of minds on this subject could be reached between the nations of Eastern Europe and the Western powers remains doubtful.

Basic to the disagreement between East and West in Helsinki, and at subsequent discussions in Geneva, are differing conceptions of the relationship between the individual and the state. Western delegates took the position that national boundaries should not be allowed to prevent individuals from having free access to information from abroad, and that this would help to improve understanding among nations. Delegates from Eastern Europe stressed that the state must have the right to decide what kinds of information are disseminated within its borders, and criticized Western proposals that did not concede this right as attempts to interfere in the internal affairs of other nations.

Soviet and East European spokesmen have shown particular sensitivity to the prospect that television satellites will be able to carry programs originating in one country directly to television receivers in another, and have advocated that program exchanges be regulated by treaty: "The conclusion of international agreements on exchanges of broadcast programs is the most acceptable means of controlling and combating harmful and illegal broadcasts." (Kolosov, 1972.) When democratic governments point out that they cannot control the content of private media, the answer sometimes is that private media do not in actuality exist and that "so-called 'private' mass information organizations" in reality represent the governments of the nations in which they are located. (Kolosov, 1973, p. 58.)

The sensitivity of the Eastern powers to shortwave radio broadcasts originating outside their borders has been evident for many years. Denunciations of foreign broadcasts have been frequent, and some of the stations involved have been jammed continuously and others sporadically. A British broadcaster has expressed the opinion that one of the Eastern powers' objectives at the Conference on Security and Cooperation in Europe has been to arrive at a convention on exchange of information with the Western powers that will have the effect of limiting the content of such Western broadcasts. (Latey, 1973.)

Even though it is unlikely that far-reaching agreements governing international communication will be reached in discussions among states that have very different political philosophies, the discussions are worth continuing. They may lead to limited agreements, for instance, on the definition of certain terms; even if they do not achieve this, they will make each party better acquainted with ways of communicating more meaningfully with the other parties concerned.

Indeed, numerous limited agreements on the flow of information between nations with very different constitutional arrangements have already been reached. The United States and various Eastern European countries have for many years had agreements for the exchange of scholars as well as motion pictures and other cultural materials, and it is possible that these agreements could be broadened without either side compromising its principles. A Yugoslav proposal to the subcommittee on information of the Conference on Security and Cooperation in Europe included a number of points that appeared to be viewed favorably by both Eastern and Western delegates. One of these provided for improved access to official sources of information for foreign journalists; another called for periodic meetings of heads of government information departments to promote further cooperation. If efforts are constantly made to broaden the scope of limited agreements, it is probable that the quantity and quality of international communication can be increased significantly.

Some influence toward improving the quality of international communication might be exercised by governments on a unilateral basis. Whenever, in international discussions, a slogan or epithet is used, a governmental spokesman might immediately request clarification. Let us suppose that the U.S. representative accused another delegate of engaging in "mere propaganda." The accused would be entitled to respond, "You have said that I was conducting propaganda. I do not know how you define this. If you will tell me exactly what it is to which you object, perhaps we can do something about it."

Similarly, the United States could ask for clarification if it were alleged to be acting in an imperialist fashion: "Exactly what do you mean? If your intention is to say that American investments in a certain part of the world are too large, let us discuss that subject."

Since statements by governments and government officials are constantly echoed by the mass media and form the basis for a significant portion of international communication, it is important that their quality be high. Anything that can be done to improve their quality—whether by the power of example, by diplomatic negotiation, or by the pressure of public opinion—would contribute to understanding among nations. When words are used to obscure meaning rather than to clarify it, the chances for adjustment of differences are necessarily diminished.

Governments also can be of assistance in seeing that mass communication is able to fulfill one of its major functions more efficiently—that of providing early warning of dangerous situations. The media will be able to do this with a higher degree of effectiveness than is now the case if the government follows the policy of releasing as much as possible of the raw information that it takes in through its widespread intelligence net, and if it develops mechanisms for ensuring that its official communications are as complete and candid as possible.

Again, a multistage process would be involved. Raw information and government policy statements would be analyzed by area research institutes and other specialists who would make their findings available to the mass media; the mass media would then focus attention on the necessity for finding solutions.

This cycle is particularly important in view of the frequency with which low-level government officials are aware of dangerous situations because of their familiarity with raw intelligence, but at the same time are unable to bring these situations to the attention of higher officials because of the difficulty of penetrating the bureaucratic layers between them and the policy-makers who are able to take action. Or higher officials may not want to know about a dangerous situation because it is politically inexpedient for them to do anything about it. In such cases the mass media can short-circuit bureaucratic channels.

Sometimes they can capture the attention of higher officials directly; sometimes they can alert members of Congress or the public, who in turn will be able to enlist the attention of the executive branch.

Even if the executive branch is unable or unwilling to take immediate action on a dangerous situation that is brought to its attention, the fact that interested parties in and outside the government have been alerted to it is likely to mean that it will be dealt with more effectively. Those with expertise in the area will at least have been informed, and a wider range of possible solutions will be available for consideration when action finally becomes unavoidable.

Examples of cases where low-level government officials were aware of dangerous situations long before these situations were squarely faced are not hard to find. During the Korean War, U.S. personnel in Korea were aware of Chinese intervention at least several months before this became public knowledge. Some high Washington officials may have known about this but many did not, even within the State Department. If the U.S. military headquarters in Tokyo learned about the presence of Chinese military personnel, it sought to downgrade the importance of this fact by interpreting it as a series of isolated instances. As one student of the Korean War puts it, "the Chinese threat to intervene was in part dependent on international communication channels that, in fact, failed to work." (Whiting, 1960, pp. 171-72.)

Similarly, government personnel in Washington who monitor economic indicators started to talk about the U.S. balance of payments problem in the early 1950s, yet the problem was not directly faced for many years. And low-level officials who regularly read captured North Vietnamese documents in Vietnam during the 1960s were aware that Hanoi had no intention of settling the Vietnam war through negotiations at that time, yet higher officials continued to hold out hopes of an early negotiated settlement.

Greater government openness is only one of the the requirements for an early-warning system, but it is an important one. By making more raw information and low level analyses available to scholars and the media, the government can help to ensure that all those who might be able to contribute to the solution of particular problems have an opportunity to do so—and not only those who happen to be in the civil service or in a particular administration.

Governments have on occasion made use of communication in conjunction with negotiation or other mechanisms for the attainment of peaceful solutions. Sometimes the press has been used to signal intentions prior to negotiation, or to indicate that a government believes the time is ripe for negotiation. The Soviets are widely believed to have used this device to bring about conversations that resulted in the end of the Berlin blockade of 1948-49. (Acheson, 1969, pp. 352ff.) Or officially inspired news reports can serve to supplement secret exchanges in negotiations already in progress. Moscow appears to have done this at least twice in the arms control negotiations with the United States during 1971. (New York Times, May 23 and July 8, 1971.) In both instances, Soviet attitudes toward the negotiations were indicated by articles in Pravda or Izvestia, from which the Times picked up the story.

Publicity also may be used by a government to bring pressure on other parties to a negotiation, as was done by President Nixon when he revealed that Hanoi had not responded to a U.S. offer to fix a date for withdrawal from Vietnam. (New York Times, January 26, 1972.) The mass media were utilized in a somewhat similar manner by Lenin when he insisted that the proceedings at the Brest-Litovsk negotiations between Russia and the Central Powers be carried by radio. (Martin, 1958, p. 7.)

Although numerous examples of governmental use of public communication in conjunction with negotiation can be found, remarkably little is known about it. One reason for this is that past negotiations have never been studied from this point of view. Such studies would indeed be difficult since most records of negotiation have been confined to the texts of formal exchanges, sometimes supplemented by the recollections of some of the participants. And, as has often been pointed out, what goes on in formal negotiating sessions may be unimportant when compared with off-the-record conversations, subtle pressure on the negotiators, and strategy conferences attended by the members of only one delegation. (Academy for Educational Development, 1971.)

Thus, one way that governments could assist in the further development of communication as an instrument for use in conjunction with negotiation, mediation, and so on would be to arrange for more complete records to be compiled. These records should give particular attention to the role played by the mass media and the influence of public opinion.

Another way that governments could assist in the development of communication as a tool for use in connection with diplomatic mechanisms of conflict resolution would be to ensure that communication specialists are a party to as many of these negotiations as possible. Press officers are usually assigned to any delegation taking part in major international discussions, but their role is defined mainly as providing selected information to the press corps. Ideally, the press officer should be included in all the strategy conferences of the delegation and should actively search out opportunities for using his own communication skills to bring the negotiation to a successful conclusion.

Unfortunately, at present the social sciences can offer little guidance to such a press officer. He would have to rely largely on his own resourcefulness until such time as further research on communication and negotiation begins to generate principles that could be applied in particular situations. Nevertheless, studies of the negotiating process itself have led to a few generalizations that probably would apply to publicity about negotiations. For instance, the parties concerned are most likely to reach a satisfactory agreement if neither one resorts to threats. But if one party does issue a threat, a prompt and firm rejoinder is more likely to facilitate ultimate agreement than a conciliatory response. (Shure, Meeker, and Hansford, 1965.) Or, the more technical the discussion of an issue, the less likely the issue is to become politicized and emotionally charged. (W. L. Gould, 1968, p. 293.) Or again, a favorable climate for an arms control agreement is more likely to prevail when both sides see each other as of equal power than when one sees the other as either superior or inferior. (Walton et al., January 1969, p. 41.) Further, a number of analyses of the use of the mass media for signaling in international relations are available. (Jervis, 1970.) While these do not attempt to formulate general rules, they at least present a number of alternative modes of communication that can be considered under varying circumstances.

It is sometimes thought that the United States is at a disadvantage when it comes to diplomatic signaling since the government does not have an official or even semi-official news organ at its disposal, while most other governments do. Yet the background news conference, at which reporters agree to cite only "a high official source" or a "State Department spokesman," serves much the same purpose. Through this means, the U.S. government can advance suggestions or proposals without making them official negotiating positions. Journalists have frequently denounced background conferences, maintaining that this is one way the government uses the press to launch trial balloons without taking official responsibility. But whatever the merits or demerits of such conferences, to do away with them would remove a capability for signaling that could be of value in connection with international negotiations.

THE DESIRABILITY OF A NATIONAL INFORMATION POSTURE

Perhaps the most effective use a government can make of communication in the advancement of international understanding is to promote a climate or mood in which peaceful solutions are more likely to be reached by national leaders, accepted by national publics, and supported over time.

All means of communication available to governments can play a constructive part in this endeavor. In the United States the principal channels consist of statements by high officials and policy documents, both of which are likely to be given wide play by the commercial information media. Subsidiary channels are provided by the USIA and other government agencies that communicate directly with foreign audiences, such as the Agency for International Development and various military information offices. In addition, through its leadership role and its ability to facilitate or inhibit the activities of groups and individuals in touch with the peoples of other nations, the government can help to open new channels.

The United States has formulated policies governing the operations of the USIA but has never formed an explicit policy applying to all government communications to foreign nations. It has a military posture and an economic posture, but no information posture. That is, there are no general principles against which the practices of any particular spokesman or agency engaging in direct or indirect communication with foreign publics can be tested, as there are in the case of military or economic activities. Such guidelines are highly desirable if the government is to use its information capabilities to foster a mood favorable to the establishment and maintenance of international understanding.

Current policies applying to the USIA's output are straightforward and unobjectionable as far as they go. As summarized by its deputy director in 1971, the USIA's basic task is to advance the interests of the United States abroad. It does this by providing information about the country and its policies, by countering misinformation, and by trying to persuade foreign audiences to have respect for and confidence in the United States. (H. L. Loomis, 1971.) Much the same picture was given in a "fact sheet" distributed by the USIA's public information office in 1970: "The role of the Agency is to support the foreign policy of the United States by explaining it to people in other countries; to build overseas understanding of United States institutions and culture; and to advise the U.S. government on public opinion abroad and its implications for U.S. policy." International peace is not explicitly mentioned as a goal in these statements, but it is referred to in a presidential memorandum of January 25, 1963, which is included in a handbook for USIA employees:

> Agency activities should . . . encourage constructive
> public support abroad for the goal of a "peaceful world
> community of free and independent states, free to choose
> their own future and their own system so long as it does
> not threaten the freedom of others." [United States In-
> formation Agency, 1969.]

Examination of successive issues of the Review of Operations, issued by the USIA every six months, confirms that most of its effort is devoted to providing information about the United States and its activities. Major attention is devoted to such subjects as the space program, measures to combat poverty and discrimination, and presidential elections, as well as specific foreign policy issues.

The policies governing the USIA appear to be directed toward building a favorable, or at least not inaccurate, image of the United States and its policies, but they provide few clues to the kind of international atmosphere the government would like to promote through its communications. Nor do they suggest how such an atmosphere might be created. Of course policies guiding the USIA would not necessarily apply to other elements of government in any case, but one would assume that if an overall information policy were available it would at least be reflected in the branch of government specifically concerned with communicating with overseas audiences.

What appears to be desirable is a government-wide commitment to the establishment of an atmosphere conducive to the peaceful solution of international differences. This orientation would necessarily apply to actions as well as words. The closest thing to such a government-wide orientation in peacetime was President Franklin D. Roosevelt's "good neighbor" policy toward Latin America. Even though this policy may not have been rigorously followed at all times, it at least provided a rough yardstick against which the appropriateness of any action or statement could be measured. In the first and second world wars an even more widely applicable test was available: Will it help win the war?

To elaborate the details of an information policy designed to promote a mood favorable to conflict resolution will require years of trial and error. Nevertheless, a few components are reasonably clear. Government efforts to increase the quantity and quality of international communication, as suggested above, would be one important component. Improvement of two-way communication would be especially significant, as would the avoidance of slogans and bombast. A government would have to make particular efforts to establish its willingness to consult and to listen.

More specifically, official communications directed abroad should emphasize common values the United States shares with other nations. This has frequently been done in the past, but usually as a result of the initiative and insight of a particular official rather than as a response to policy guidelines.* It is not always easy to do, since

----

*However, a policy directive from President John F. Kennedy to the USIA did specify that it should "emphasize the ways in which

divisive factors are newsworthy and surface readily while common values often remain unstated. The wise communicator searches out the subjects that are of concern both to him and to his audience. To talk about peace and freedom when addressing a country where a large proportion of the population is hungry, for example, makes little sense. Such audiences are more interested in social justice and economic development. (White, 1967.)

A related emphasis should be on the positive aspects of diversity. One of the most effective ways of demonstrating an appreciation for diversity might be through policies toward domestic minorities. Researchers have repeatedly found that individuals who have experienced successful intercultural contacts in their own countries are more likely to have smooth relationships when they go abroad than those whose experiences have been confined mainly to a single social or ethnic group. (Cleveland, Mangone, and Adams, 1960.) As one pair of scholars puts it, "enlargement of contact and cooperation must begin at home." (Buchanan and Cantril, 1953, p. 101.) It would seem reasonable that the same principle would apply to nations: Those that are recognized as appreciating cultural diversity at home will enjoy smoother relations with states that have a different cultural character.

The United States has numerous opportunities to demonstrate its appreciation for cultural diversity. As a gesture of respect for Spanish-speaking Americans, for instance, more emphasis could be placed on the Spanish language and the traditions of Spanish-speaking countries in American schools of several cities and states.* In other areas, a similar emphasis could be given to Italian, Polish, French, German, Chinese, Japanese, or Scandinavian languages. The opportunities for recognizing the rich cultures of Africa, of which traces have been preserved among black Americans, are almost limitless. While control of education is a local matter, the federal government could exercise a powerful influence through some device such as a "second language program" in the U.S. Office of Education. However it is conveyed, the message that cultural diversity is appreciated

---

United States policies harmonize with those of other peoples and governments . . . ." (New York Times, October 29, 1963.)

*Establishing respect for diversity is not easy. Some ten years ago, the writer attempted to persuade the New York Transit Authority to put up car cards in Spanish in New York City subways so that all New Yorkers could learn at least a few words of Spanish. The response from one Transit Authority official was, "We have enough trouble teaching everybody to speak English." Since then, apparently in response to other pressures, Spanish-language advertisements have appeared in subway cars, along with a few public service messages.

would seem to be an important one for establishing an atmosphere conducive to the peaceful resolution of international differences.

Government communications also should be shaped with a view to avoiding the creation or strengthening of a mood of crisis, either at home or abroad. While the press may on occasion dramatize international disputes, thereby giving the public a sense that an emergency exists, official pronouncements play an important part in either fueling or dampening the flames. An analysis of U.G. government behavior in six international disputes following World War II concluded, "The more experienced an Administration, the less likely it is to make an early proclamation of crisis . . . ." (W. L. Gould, 1968, p. 300.) There will be instances when a government will feel it has to alert the public to a dangerous situation in order to mobilize domestic support, but the longer a crisis atmosphere can be avoided the more likely it is that a wide range of possible solutions will be considered and that a climate favorable to peaceful discussion will prevail.

Particular attention should be given to preserving and reinforcing the favorable attitudes toward peaceful conflict resolution that already exist between certain nations. While communication can be an effective instrument for reinforcing existing favorable attitudes, it is usually unable to change unfavorable ones that have already been established. Government spokesmen should make special efforts to address themselves to nations with which relations are good; to ensure that communications are used to preserve an atmosphere conducive to the resolution of differences that may arise. Leaders of many countries have complained with considerable justification that they are ignored by the United States as long as there is no significant dispute between them and Washington. Much more of the government communication capability should be used to prevent differences with these countries from becoming acute, rather than for smoothing over problems that have already become serious. This does not necessarily mean that USIA operations in such areas as Western Europe, Japan, and Australia should be expanded; it may be sufficient for government spokesmen to make clear in the course of their day-to-day activities that the United States places a high value on good relations with these nations and is constantly searching for ways in which the ties of good feeling can be made even closer.

A related situation in which communication can be effective is in following up and reinforcing an international agreement that has already been reached. As a senior member of the United Nations secretariat observed recently, nobody seems to care about a problem after a compromise has been reached. The diplomats simply go on to the next problem. This leaves the way clear for tensions to form again and for new differences to arise. In such situations communication channels can be used to monitor how well an agreement is working and to keep the way open for any necessary adjustments.

A social scientist with long experience in Washington has suggested to the writer that the tendency to ignore nations with which
relations are good is especially strong in the U.S. government because
of the large number of official posts occupied by lawyers. The legal
expert is accustomed to thinking on a "case" basis. He applies himself diligently to one case until it is settled; then he closes the books
on that one and goes on to another. (Members of the legal profession
will be quick to recognize that this criticism, unsupported by evidence,
may be classified as hearsay. If the shoe doesn't fit, they should feel
free to throw it out of court.) In any event, international relations
parallel life in a community much more than the proceedings in a
court of law. One cannot establish a working arrangement with one
neighbor and then turn one's back on him while negotiating with a
second. Constant awareness of the interests of all neighbors is required, and one of the most effective ways to maintain such awareness
is through communication.

In building an international atmosphere of trust, what a government says to the citizens of its own country is especially important
since such statements are likely to be interpreted by foreign observers
as a more accurate indication of government attitudes than propaganda
directed abroad. Furthermore, in an open society such as the United
States, government communications to domestic audiences are easily
picked up by the commercial news media and publicized in other
countries. And remarks occasioned by domestic political necessity
may be misinterpreted abroad. As one research report notes with
reference to arms control, "merely to reduce the criticism and opposition of those who stress national security may require a military
posture and defiant statements that can mislead the adversary."
(Walton et al., January 1969, p. 17.)

No satisfactory solution to this problem has been proposed, but
it can at least be minimized by an awareness on the part of government
officials that foreign as well as domestic audiences should be taken
into account whenever public statements are made. (Stone, 1967, pp.
135ff.)

Communications on foreign policy subjects that are directed to
domestic audiences offer certain advantages as well as problems. A
psychiatrist has pointed out that one way to reassure a suspicious
patient is to allow him to overhear the doctor discussing his case
with someone else. (Frank, 1968, p. 237.) The same principle seems
to hold in relations among nations. A number of observers have noted
that some individuals in other countries place more trust in the English-
language news broadcasts of the Armed Forces Television and Radio
Service that are directed at U.S. personnel overseas than they do in
Voice of America broadcasts that are beamed to them in their own
language. One might expect that the same would be true of domestic

American communications that are picked up and carried to other countries by international wire services. These, too, might contribute toward an atmosphere in which international differences could more easily be resolved.

In addition, governments could use their communication capabilities to mobilize, or at least to put in touch with one another, those who are seriously concerned with the advancement of international understanding. Many governments, including that of the United States, are already doing this to a very considerable extent. Often overlooked, because it is so obvious, is the fact that increased speed and ease of travel, combined with a plethora of international conferences, is helping to forge closer personal relationships among the leading foreign policy personnel of many nations. One scholar has observed that foreign ministers now have so many opportunities for face-to-face contact that they are forming a new international elite, in a sense replacing the old international aristocracy with its intermarriage and shared social life. (Modelski, 1970.) At the same time, diplomats at international conferences and at the United Nations are, in effect, creating their own encounter groups and T-groups through corridor gossip and informal exchanges at cocktail parties and receptions. They are learning to communicate more effectively, if not necessarily more fully.

Exchange programs sponsored by governments often do much the same thing. They make it possible for professionals and other specialists to become acquainted with those with similar interests in other countries, to communicate across national borders, and sometimes to develop common points of view. To the extent that a government wishes to make use of exchange programs specifically to help build groups of people interested in increasing international understanding, it should impose somewhat different criteria of selection than the ones usually used at present. Exchanges are usually chosen on the basis that an opportunity to travel or work abroad will further their own professional interests or add to professional expertise in their own country; possible benefits to good relations among the nationalities involved are recognized but are secondary. Thus a large proportion of international exchanges are natural scientists, engineers, and administrators. This mode of exchange is valuable and should be continued, but additional emphasis could be placed on involving persons who are in a position to interpret one society to another, who have a commitment to improving international relations, or who happen to be experts on issues that are currently dividing the countries concerned. Some persons in these categories have always taken part in exchange programs, including journalists, politicians, and political scientists. The only point to be made here is that, if exchanges are to be used to build a corps of persons concerned with international understanding, they should be arranged with this end in view and exchangees should be given opportunities for sustained interchange with their opposite numbers in other countries.

A model for the use of conferences of private citizens to attack problems dividing two or more nations is provided by the Pugwash and Dartmouth conferences, where specialists from a number of countries have had an opportunity to discuss such questions as arms control, nuclear energy, and foreign trade. (The Dartmouth conferences have involved only U.S. and Soviet personnel; Pugwash conferences have included individuals from a number of countries in both the Eastern and Western blocs.) These conferences have been sponsored mainly by private foundations and there is some question as to whether governmental sponsorship would be appropriate. But there are other cases where government involvement would not inhibit discussion or where governments could facilitate conferences arranged by third parties. The writer would particularly like to see a series of multinational conferences of retired foreign service officers, at which outstanding world problems could be discussed.

Governments also could play a role in creating permanent institutions devoted to improving relations among nations. Thirty years ago the public relations specialist Edward L. Bernays proposed the establishment of a U.S.-Canadian Joint Board for Mutual Understanding, composed of fourteen individuals, seven from each country. Each side would appoint, for life, two elder statesmen, a social psychologist, a media expert, an educator, an advertiser, and a public relations expert. The board would then operate two bureaus of information, one in each country. (Bernays, 1943.) There are obviously many possible variations on this theme, but few have been explored. The "friendship societies" established by the Soviet Union to hyphenate itself to almost every other country may provide some valuable experience. Although widely believed by Western scholars to constitute mainly an arm of Soviet diplomacy, these societies have at least experimented with some modes of international communication that are little known in other countries. (Nemzer, 1949.)

The libraries and information centers operated by the U.S. and many other governments throughout the world could play an active part in forming contacts among those interested in the peaceful resolution of international issues. At present, most such centers emphasize providing information about the sponsoring country to citizens of other countries. This function is important but it could be supplemented by greater efforts to serve as meeting points and address bureaus for those interested in building a more peaceful world.

Mass media operated by governments likewise have served mainly as conveyor belts for information about the sponsoring country. They, too, could place more emphasis on linking individuals and groups

105

in different nations. This could be done by providing greater coverage of organizations devoted to the solution of international problems and by providing a mail address that could be used by individuals throughout the world who wanted to get in touch with these organizations.

For instance, an Arms Control Association was organized in the United States in 1971. The Voice of America and some of the printed materials issued by the USIA could describe the activities of this association. Some individuals abroad might wish to get in touch with it; others might see the possibility of organizing similar associations in their own countries. Coverage also could be given to groups concerned with ecological problems, trade problems, border disputes, and so on. Panel discussions could be arranged, featuring representatives from various national organizations. In this way, relatively small groups and powerless individuals could gradually be forged into larger organizations or bodies of public opinion that would have a greater influence on the course of international events. Again, some activities of this type are already being conducted by the USIA, the State Department, and other agencies. The issue is one of ensuring greater emphasis, a more systematic approach, and increased ingenuity.

Governments can do a great deal to expand the role of mass communication in the advancement of international understanding. Whether they will do this, or the consistency with which they will do it, is open to question. When the interests of a particular government conflict with the requirements for a more peaceful world, it is probable that the former will prevail. If it is a question of staying in power or advancing some important national interest, a government may choose to violate all the principles of communication suggested above: It may restrict information, resort to rabble-rousing slogans, cover up dangerous situations, oppose peaceful solutions, seek to heighten a crisis atmosphere, and try to prevent its citizens from forming associations with like-minded people abroad. The realities of power politics will frequently oppose the improvement of international understanding.

But frequently they will not. Every effort should be made to ensure that the enormous resources of governments are used constructively. The task of finding ways for the peaceful resolution of international differences is too important to be left to governments alone, but they can be powerful allies.

8

THE UNITED NATIONS:
THE STILL, SMALL VOICE

Like the voice of conscience, the information program of the United Nations is weak in decibels and frequently unheard but has great potential influence. While underfinanced, understaffed, and subject to stringent political limitations, it nevertheless has developed into a worldwide network that can perform functions beyond the capacity of any other information service. It enjoys better access to some nations than do most other foreign information services, it benefits from the prestige of the world body that sponsors it, and it is a truly international undertaking.

THE SCOPE AND LIMITATIONS OF
U.N. PUBLIC INFORMATION

The limited scope of the U.N. Office of Public Information (OPI) is evident from its history and budget. In 1948 it was authorized expenditures of approximately $4 million; by 1971 its budget had grown to $9.2 million, but during the same period the budget of the United Nations itself had increased fivefold. The proportion of funds devoted to information has declined from more than 10 percent of the total U.N. budget to 4.6 percent. In size, the U.N. information program is comparable to that of a small or middle-sized power; it is only about one-twentieth the size of the programs maintained by the United States and the Soviet Union.

Within these stringent financial limitations, the OPI conducts information activities of surprising extent. It issues about 3,500 press releases each year from its offices in New York, and some 15,000 press releases worldwide if one includes various language editions and local releases prepared by the offices outside the United States.

It publishes a number of books and periodicals describing U.N. operations. It offers a wide range of radio and television services to national information media. It operates 52 information centers throughout the world. It also maintains a Center for Economic and Social Information that disseminates materials of a more specialized nature in support of the Second United Nations Development Decade.

In addition, international organizations affiliated with the United Nations engage in fairly extensive public information and educational activities. These include UNESCO, the World Health Organization, the Food and Agriculture Organization, and others. All of these bodies issue publications and press releases and sponsor international conferences. It is difficult, and probably pointless, to estimate how much money they devote to "information" as contrasted with "education." As a rough guess it might be concluded that their combined information programs approximate in size that of the OPI. But since each of the specialized organizations deals only with its particular field of interest and is not subject to policies established by the Office of Public Information, their combined capacity cannot realistically be added to that of the OPI.

The most powerful communication capability of the United Nations lies in the secretary-general, rather than in the OPI or any of the specialized agencies. What the secretary-general says is news in all parts of the world. He can command attention in the same way as the chief executive of a major power. But his words are subject to many of the same political limitations as the OPI's releases.

Policies governing the OPI were established by a General Assembly resolution passed in 1946 and reaffirmed, with minor modifications, by successive resolutions since then. The major goal of U.N. publicity is to promote understanding throughout the world of the work and purposes of the organization. In pursuing this goal, the OPI is enjoined to rely primarily on existing public and private information services, to refrain from propaganda, and to pay particular attention to regions where information services are less well developed. In the words of a recent U.N. document, the OPI plays essentially a "supporter" role, which is "required by its very character as an organization run by and for sovereign states . . . ." (United Nations, 1971, pp. 11-12.) The OPI currently has a limited capacity to develop its own themes and communicate them directly to audiences throughout the world. In general, it must stress the themes enunciated by the General Assembly and other U.N. agencies, and it must rely mainly on the correspondents covering the United Nations and on national and private information services to disseminate its communications.

Even so, this charter is a broad one. In the political field, the OPI has been directed to give the "widest possible dissemination of information to such diverse activities as those relating to disarmament, decolonization . . . , the promotion of friendly relations among peoples and countries, the evils of apartheid, human rights, status of women, rights of children, treatment of prisoners in South Africa, the work of the International Law Commission and the International Court of Justice, the dangers of a possible nuclear war, the protection of minorities and the promotion of the ideals of peace among youth, etc." (United Nations, 1971, p. 13.)

Coverage of the United Nations by the world's news media is spotty. While the international wire services and major newspaper and broadcasting enterprises have permanent reporters at U.N. headquarters, most of the nations of the world are not represented by their own correspondents. The five big wire services supply more than 59 percent of all international news copy emanating from the headquarters, but they cannot cover many U.N. activities because these are not sufficient interest to most of their customers. The Third World is particularly poorly served. At a major discussion of African problems in 1968, the 32 African nations brought more than 160 delegates of ambassadorial rank to New York but there was only one African correspondent (from Ghana) in attendance. (Granitsas, 1970). And even if a wire service or correspondent sends a dispatch, it may not be used by the media to which it is supplied.

The OPI's shortwave radio news services might seem to be universally available. These broadcasts, transmitted over leased facilities of several national information agencies, are designed to be picked up and relayed by local stations, but only 15 countries made regular use of them as of 1971. These countries, incidentally, included widely differing political types—for example, Turkey and Poland, Thailand and Yugoslavia—leading one to suspect that non-use is not so much for political reasons as because the broadcasts are not found to be very interesting. The use of television and film services offered by the OPI depends completely on the initiative of local media, which must make arrangements for procuring the footage they want.

While the 52 United Nations information centers have a more assured capability of reaching audiences in countries they serve, they must be operated with circumspection. As of 1969, no bilateral agreement existed between a host country and the U.N. secretariat with regard to these centers. This meant that the contractual obligations of both parties had not been spelled out. Instead, the usual practice was for the U.N. secretariat and the host country to merely exchange letters confirming that agreement about the desirability of opening a given center had been reached. (Marjonovic and Pindic, 1969, p. 403.) From a legal standpoint, any of the centers could easily be closed by a host government at any time, although they are given some protection by the fact that they operate within the framework of General Assembly resolutions on public information and also are covered by the Convention on the Privileges and Immunities of the United Nations. However, the greatest weakness of the centers is not their legal status but that they have inadequate operational budgets and that only about two-thirds of them have professional directors recruited especially for the task. The other centers are supervised by the resident representative of the United Nations Development Program, who of course has many other duties.

SOME POTENTIAL CONTRIBUTIONS

Within the limits imposed by poverty and the nature of an organization run by sovereign governments, there are some exciting opportunities for U.N. communications to make greater contributions to international understanding. To realize these opportunities, the Office of Public Information would require only a slightly larger budget. As little as two or three million additional dollars would make possible a much greater impact.

The United Nations could make a modest but worthwhile contribution toward increasing the quantity of international communication. The OPI is in an excellent position to serve as an impartial adviser to news media with regard to international coverage. Especially the poorer media and those in less developed parts of the world would welcome more attention from U.N. headquarters. For instance, the OPI could ensure that editors were aware of information sources available to them without cost or at very low cost. These might include shortwave broadcasts, materials distributed by national governments, new releases from private research organizations in such fields as education and health, and services offered by the United Nations and its affiliated organizations. These and other advisory functions could be carried out in conjunction with international organizations of journalists, publishers, broadcasters, and other communication specialists, many of which already have ties to the United Nations.

The most important way the United Nations could stimulate increased international exchange of information would be through agreements facilitating the free flow of news. These agreements would have to be concluded among the governments concerned, but the U.N. secretariat, again in an advisory capacity, could point out areas in which agreements were possible and its initiative might be welcomed by all concerned.

Direct contributions of the United Nations toward a greater flow of international communications also would be desirable, but more than a slight increment would probably be impossible for both financial and political reasons. One proposal that would not involve greatly increased expenditures would be more frequent "state of the world" addresses by the secretary-general. These would find their way into most of the world's newspapers and broadcast facilities. Another proposal is that U.N. members commit themselves to devote one hour per week of prime broadcast time to U.N.-produced programs. (Gardner, 1969.) A more ambitious idea is that the United Nations might organize an international press agency that would collect and disseminate news about international relations. (Popovic, 1969, pp. 90-91.) Many observers of the United Nations have noted that it would be desirable to increase the personnel and resources at U.N. information centers.

The Office of Public Information and other U.N. agencies concerned with communication have an unusual opportunity to promote improved quality of international information. Nevertheless, although the opportunity is there, it will be difficult to realize because of the intellectual problems involved. In theory, the OPI could provide the world's editors with a model of how to report thorny international issues in an impartial manner, without the use of slogans, stereotypes, and invective—and at the same time to present this information in such a way that large audiences would find it interesting. Similarly, the OPI could raise the quality of world journalism if it could find a way to provide lively accounts of dull and technical—but very important —negotiations and decisions. As a conference on the United Nations of the Next Decade put it, "the United Nations and its members must also do more to present its achievements and challenges in ways that will command the attention and imagination of mankind." (Stanley Foundation, 1969.)

Achievement of a lively style has long been one of the challenges faced by journalists working for the United Nations. As Le Journal de Genève complained on May 8, 1972, the rule in international organizations is never to ruffle the feelings of the member-states and to smooth over contentious issues. As a result, "papers written by these unfortunate journalists are about as spicy as boiled rice. . . . Realities and life disappear with them."

How to ensure fairness and make difficult subjects interesting are problems that have long confounded journalists of many nations; they will never be completely solved by the OPI. Nevertheless, the desirability of making as much progress as possible toward solving them points to a relatively simple decision. This is that, within the limits of budgetary tolerance, emphasis should be placed on quality in the preparation of press releases and other materials. (The importance of OPI press releases rests partially on their wide distribution. Each release is produced in a minimum of 1,200 copies. Of

these, 400 go to correspondents at U.N. headquarters, 650 to various
national delegations, and 150 to U.N. information centers around the
world. Many of those distributed to delegations also find their way
to media back home.) In practical terms, this might mean issuing
fewer releases and publication, allowing more time for the preparation of each, and experimenting with different forms of presentation.

The OPI is in a unique position for such experimentation. Since
its staff includes skilled journalists from several countries, and since
professional personnel from practically all other countries are easily
available, it could test out information materials for both interest
and fairness more efficiently than any other organization in the world.

Improvement in the quality of OPI's own output would lead to
increased utilization of this output throughout the world, but even
more important is the cumulative effect it would be likely to have
on information handling by others. If OPI were able to establish a
standard of quality for international journalism that achieved wide
recognition, it would soon find emulators in many countries.

The mass communication capabilities at the United Nations,
combined with the more than 100 field offices and observation points
it maintains throughout the world, offer an excellent basis for an
effective early warning system. The U.N. secretariat could ensure
that a wide variety of dangerous situations, as well as opportunities
for positive action to cement peace, are called to the attention of
those able to act on them.

There have been a number of proposals looking toward the
strengthening of the U.N. observation system. For instance, a White
House Conference on International Cooperation in 1965 suggested the
recruitment of a U.N. Peace Observation Corps that would be available
to the secretary-general: "Its main function would be to focus the
eyes of the international organized community on a situation which
if ignored could endanger the peace." (White House Conference on
International Cooperation, 1965, p. 30.)

Similarly, a panel of the American Association for the United
Nations recommended in 1971 that a U.N. Fact Finding Center be
established. It would be designed to provide the world body with the
capability of responding promptly in situations threatening peace and
security, to monitor cease-fire agreements, and to analyze potential
conflict situations. (United Nations Association—U.S.A., 1971b.)

Even without the creation of new instrumentalities, the capabilities of the U.N. secretariat to monitor the international situation
are appreciable. At any point in time are likely to be U.N. peace-
keeping forces, mediators, and truce observers in many parts of the
world. In addition, there are the U.N. information centers and special
representatives. All these individuals and bodies are in touch with
headquarters. Specialized agencies of the United Nations maintain

even more offices, which may be concerned with development assistance, education, health, disaster relief, or other matters. While not all these offices are in direct touch with U.N. headquarters in New York, their reports are available to the U.N. secretariat and direct contact would be easy to establish. Furthermore, the U.N. charter gives the secretary-general fairly wide powers of investigation and observation. As the servant of 135 sovereign nations he must use these powers with circumspection, but his ability to call attention to dangers and opportunities is far greater than his ability to act. (Gordenker, 1967, pp. 325-27.) It is partly for this reason that the refinement and development of the U.N. mass communication capabilities is particularly important. The secretary-general's peace-keeping role, sharply limited in other respects by national sovereignty, can be substantially enlarged through the resourceful use of the mass media.

In order to develop its early warning capacity and to link it to the activities of the Office of Public Information, the United Nations will require improved point-to-point communication facilities. There have been several recommendations to the effect that satellites should be enlisted for this purpose. (United Nations Association—U.S.A. 1971b.) However they are to be provided, better point-to-point communications are urgently needed. During the Congo crisis, for instance, at one point U.N. headquarters was out of touch with its field commanders for 24 hours because of atmospheric interference with shortwave facilities. Even when communications have not broken down, serious delays have been frequent. (d'Arcy, 1970.)

Those concerned about the capacity, speed, and reliability of U.N. point-to-point communications usually think in terms of administrative efficiency. This is important, but good communication is equally vital for the United Nations in its performance of the early warning function. If he is to use the organization's information capabilities to call attention to dangerous situations, or to unusual opportunities, the secretary-general will require complete and prompt reports from field installations.

The United Nations has a unique opportunity to activate and mobilize those interested in finding peaceful solutions to international problems. It also can help to build world public opinion favoring peaceful solutions. This opportunity to mobilize people of good will and foster world public opinion on critical issues is based on the United Nation's character as a supranational organization freed from the incubus of national interest, and on its ability to command the attention of politically inclined people throughout the world. Psychologists have pointed out that, just as unstructured training groups in psychotherapy require a "superordinate leader" if they are to function efficiently, the nations composing the unstructured international community need such a leader. (Appelbaum 1967.) While the U.N. secretary-general is severely limited as to his powers of action, he can still provide a measure of superordinate leadership.

One of the major functions of a leader, whether of a small group or a community of nations, is to focus the attention of all members on certain common problems. There have been a number of proposals that the United Nations should do this with respect to international disarmament and the arms race. The former Belgian minister of foreign affairs has suggested on several occasions that the General Assembly might prepare an information campaign on the significance of the arms race for the peoples of the world, and that the secretary-general should then take the steps to ensure wide dissemination of this information in all member-states. (Larock, 1970.) A somewhat similar recommendation has been made by the Committee on Foreign Affairs of the U.S. House of Representatives: namely, that the United Nations "consider the possibility of monitoring and giving maximum public disclosure to the continuing arms race in conventional and other weapons." (Committee on Foreign Affairs, 1971.) Population control is another issue on which it has been suggested that the United Nations should help to focus world attention. (United Nations Association—U.S.A., 1969.)

Progress toward determining a number of problems to be given priority attention was made in 1972 when the secretary-general directed that the OPI set up a work program "based on the principal information themes that are of concern to the United Nations." Specifically, four themes were chosen for emphasis in 1973 and 1974: disarmament, the Second United Nations Development Decade, human rights, and decolonization. These subjects were to be dealt with in "a series of well-thoughtout and coordinated multimedia, information strategies." (United Nations, 1972.)

How well the new approach will work out remains to be seen, The chosen themes are broad ones and were selected in response to resolutions of the General Assembly and other U.N. organs. It would be desirable for the general themes to be supplemented by a list of more specific issues and problems. This might be done by maintaining surveillance of principal news media throughout the world or by international public opinion polling, or both, as well as by drawing on reports from U.N. field offices. A selection of items from this list could then be made.

However the agenda of questions and problems is compiled, it should be fairly short and should be brought to the attention of as many as possible of those in a position to influence solutions either directly or indirectly. One method for doing this, preparation of periodic reports by the Secretary-General on the state of the world, has already been mentioned. If broadcast media of all or most member-nations could be persuaded to carry regular programs prepared by the Office of Public Information, this would provide another means of focusing world attention on a finite number of issues at any one time.

A relatively cheap but highly effective method of ensuring that a large proportion of political leaders are made aware of outstanding problems would be the preparation of a weekly or semimonthly newsletter. This could be disseminated by airmail, or by faster means, to all principal news media and also to a carefully compiled list of influential individuals in and out of political office. Circulation of this "letter from the secretary-general" might be limited by some national governments, but it would be likely to receive a close reading by a large proportion of influential persons throughout the world.

These efforts by the United Nations to focus world attention on certain priority problems might appear unnecessary in view of the elaborate international communication network already in existence. One might assume that the editors of all major news media and political leaders in all nations would in any case be thinking about many of the same questions at any one time. But this is not the case. Repeated studies have shown that attention in each country tends to focus heavily on national problems and that at present there is no mechanism for ensuring that all political leaders and other opinion leaders have access to a common agenda of priority issues. (Davison, 1973.) Indeed, one reason world public opinion forms on so few issues is that like-minded people in different countries are rarely thinking about the same things at the same time. The United Nations could make a major contribution toward changing this situation by providing a common focus of attention. This task is already included by inference in a description of the OPI's mission by the secretary-general, which (paraphrasing Bernard Cohen) states that the Office of Public Information should not try to tell the people of the world what to think but should tell them what to think about. (United Nations, 1972, pp. 13-14.)

When it comes to using mass communication to facilitate negotiations, the United Nations is in a particularly strategic position. A large proportion of international negotiations take place at the United Nations or under its auspices. It has an opportunity to experiment with various formulas and to build up a body of experience.

The United Nations should explore the following possibilities, among others, of using its communication capabilities to encourage negotiation of outstanding issues and to bring these negotiations to successful conclusion:

- To focus attention on issues that might be partially or completely solved by the use of international negotiation.
- To confer prestige on negotiators, arbitrators, and others who seek to play the role of "third parties" in negotiations.
- To ensure that a wide variety of possible solutions are brought to the attention of negotiators, their governments, and politically interested circles in the countries concerned.

- To bring about a situation in which the mass media themselves function as "third parties"—rewarding conciliatory gestures by either side, applauding partial agreement, and urging more complete agreement.
- To encourage acceptance by the governments and publics concerned of any agreement that might be reached.
- To encourage adherence to these agreements after they are reached, keeping attention focused on them and pointing out how their observance could be strengthened to the mutual advantage of both sides.

There are many ways the United Nations could use its information capabilities to pursue such functions as these. Existing facilities, including the press releases, radio programs, and publications already being prepared, could be pressed into service. Statements by the secretary-general or a periodic newsletter from the secretary-general would probably be even more effective. A dramatic possibility would be for the Office of Public Information to make arrangements with national authorities for international radio and television hook-ups that could be activated in times of crisis and used to press for negotiations. Experts from each country involved, and from third countries, could then be asked to express their views on the crisis and to suggest possible solutions. Their specific assignment would be to develop as many constructive courses of action as possible, without being required to recommend any specific solution.

While individual nations or private parties also might make use of mass communication in this manner, the United Nations can do so with less appearance of interfering in affairs that do not concern it. The United Nations is already recognized as a meeting place "at which it is taken for granted by the international community as normal that every member, including antagonists, should be present." (Edmead, 1971, p. 32.) Mass media channels of the United Nations, or under its auspices, can serve much the same function as a meeting place for all nations.

Through its very existence, the United Nations helps to create a mood favorable to the peaceful resolution of international differences. It symbolizes the ability of nations to come together, discuss outstanding problems, and seek solutions. An important task of U.N. communications is to emphasize this symbolism—to promote acceptance of the idea that the nations of the world constitute a community and that peaceful solutions to the differences within this community can be found.

This is a huge assignment, far beyond the modest communication capabilities of the United Nations alone. Nevertheless, it can take some steps itself and can use its influence to persuade other media to cooperate. Part of the task is to ensure that the positive achievements of the United Nations itself are brought to the attention of a wide public. In the words of a report on the United Nations of the 1970s:

> The news media and information agencies should give
> more coverage to the vital non-political work of the Uni-
> ted Nations which often goes unnoticed, and should em-
> phasize the fundamental and continuing efforts and prob-
> lems of the United Nations rather than the crises of the
> moment. [Stanley Foundation, 1969.]

Building a sense of community among the peoples of the world involves much more than promoting support for the United Nations itself. At present, we have little more than common sense to guide us when it comes to using mass communications to this end. Nevertheless, this is a goal that the U.N. Office of Public Information can keep before it, a goal that can serve as one criterion for the activities of this office.

MASS COMMUNICATION AS A
NATURAL INSTRUMENT FOR THE UNITED NATIONS

On occasion, the United Nations is capable of decisive action—but only when all or most of its members agree. At other times, the organs of the United Nations, including the secretary-general and the secretariat, must rely on moral force, on persuasion, or on merely providing information. These forms of influence may be exercised through negotiation or other forms of person-to-person contact, but more commonly they depend on mass communication. For a large group or a nation to be persuaded, informed, or influenced, the mass media must usually be brought into play.

It is therefore natural that the United Nations and its affiliated agencies give great attention to mass communication in connection with their work in economic development, education, health, and other spheres. At the same time, it is surprising that greater emphasis is not placed on mass communication in connection with the primary task of the United Nations—that of conflict resolution.

Communication is an especially appropriate instrument for U.N. agencies in that it is hedged about with fewer restrictions than are most other forms of action. The secretariat is already authorized wide latitude when it comes to gathering and disseminating information. The same is true of many committees and specialized agencies. As long as the secretariat or other agency does not become an advocate of a particular point of view with which an appreciable number of members are in disagreement, it is unlikely that its authority to engage in communication will be restricted. Nor is any U.N. agency likely to be guilty of such advocacy if it makes intelligent use of communication in support of conflict resolution, since communications of this nature must in any case avoid adopting the view of any one party to a conflict. The United Nations already offers admirable facilities for discussion and negotiation; its greatest unfulfilled potential lies in the realm of mass communication.

At present we know relatively little about the role the mass media can play in conflict resolution, but this ignorance in itself is another reason why an active role by the United Nations would be desirable. More than any other institution, it is in a position to gather and centralize the knowledge gained by students and practitioners in many countries. It also can conduct its own experiments, build on its own experience, and provide a central point where the experience of others can be accumulated and analyzed. The U.N. Office of Public Information, assisted by UNITAR and such specialized agencies as UNESCO, should become not only the world's leading user of mass communication in conflict resolution but also the world's leading authority on it.

To expand the mass communication capabilities of the United Nations would require additional funds, but the supplementary budget needed is of such a small order of magnitude that it may prove difficult to gain approval for it. Hard-headed administrators and national representatives will find it difficult to believe that a more peaceful world can be purchased for a few million dollars a year. Nevertheless, this is the conclusion to which the above analysis points.

9

**COMMUNICATION IN
THE MIDDLE EAST:
AN ILLUSTRATION**

The test of the utility of observations made in the foregoing
chapters is whether any of them might be helpful in connection with
the conflict in Northern Ireland, territorial disputes in South Asia,
differences of opinion between Panama and the United States, or gentle-
manly disagreements among members of the European Common Market. Just how the mass media might facilitate conflict resolution in
any one of these situations, or in some other, can best be judged by
those with expert knowledge of the facts and factors in each case.
Since any communication must be about something, the student of
communication must yield to political and area specialists when it
comes to discussing the utility of the mass media in any particular
instance.

Our principal purpose up to this point has been to outline some
potentialities of the mass media for conflict resolution in general
and to suggest the kinds of questions the appropriate specialists might
ask in connection with individual situations. We have noted that the
media can focus attention, activate and reinforce existing attitudes,
provide a shared pool of information, publicize new alternatives, put
like-minded people in touch with each other, and so on. The media
also have the ability to reach national leaders—those who make decisions regarding war and peace—and to influence them in certain
respects. The question then remains: How are the capabilities of
mass communication to be applied to a given international dispute?

More specifically, one may ask how the quantity and quality
of information exchanged among two or more nations may be increased,
how the media might be able to call attention both to potentially dangerous situations and to opportunities for furthering international
understanding, how negotiations might be encouraged, and how bodies
of opinion and public moods favorable to conflict resolution might be

formed. And which media should be used for these purposes? Should they be private channels, should national information services play a role, or would it be preferable if the communication facilities of the United Nations were to be utilized? What kind of infrastructure would be required by these media? Where would they obtain the information that might be of utility in resolving the conflict?

In the absence of specialized area knowledge, it is presumptuous to make specific recommendations. Nevertheless, we can provide at least an illustration of how some of these questions might be asked and answered. The Middle East has been chosen for illustrative purposes precisely because it represents such a seemingly insoluble problem. If communication might help to increase the chances of a peaceful settlement of the Arab-Israeli dispute, then one could say with greater confidence that it could play a role in lowering the level of tension in almost any international conflict. As far as the content of the following suggestions is concerned, those who are more knowledgeable about the Middle East are requested to make the necessary additions and corrections as they read.

One cannot write about the Middle East without running the risk of being overtaken by events. The conflict of October 1973, in particular, introduced new factors, such as Arab use of oil as an instrument of political pressure, about the long-term effects of which one can only speculate. Nevertheless, to avoid a problem because it is difficult is also to ignore possible solutions. Therefore, it may be useful to suggest a number of courses of action, some of which might be appropriate under conditions obtaining in the future.

It would be absurd to expect that any communication strategy could, by itself, bring peace and concord to the Middle East. It would be equally absurd to assume that communication could make no difference. One of our guiding principles throughout this discussion has been that if there is any possibility that the mass media can decrease the probability of conflict and increase the likelihood of a stable situation, then this possibility is worth exploring. Since the cost of using the mass media is relatively low, even modest gains are worth striving for.

ARAB-ISRAELI COMMUNICATION PRIOR TO 1973

The state of Arab-Israeli communication has never been encouraging. There has been substantial misunderstanding on both sides. Rather than providing information that would promote peaceful solutions, dominant mass media voices have fanned feelings of fear and hostility. Individuals who favored compromise solutions have been isolated and in some cases persecuted. Government leaders leaning toward moderate positions have found little support among publics in their own countries, and may even have refrained from stating their private thoughts openly.

There have been good reasons for this situation. Few reasonable people would behave differently if they suddenly found themselves in the position of either an Israeli or an Arab editor or governmental leader. The political, social, and psychological forces bending individuals toward existing patterns of behavior on both sides of the demarcation lines have been almost impossible to resist. The problem is how—without further violence—to change the situation so that reasonable people could behave differently.

With regard to Arab-Israeli mutual misunderstanding there has been little disagreement among third-party observers. Peter Grose of the New York Times, writing in 1971 (February 28), spoke of an "information gap, an almost total inability of otherwise sophisticated people on either side to attain a perspective of detachment." In the previous year James Reston observed that the Israelis seemed not only to have closed ranks about the war but to have "closed their minds about new ways of getting out of it"; at the same time he found the Arab press conformist, propagandistic, and jingoistic. (New York Times, February 13, 1970.) A survey of communication between Israelis and Arabs conducted by Yonah Alexander during the 1968-70 period concluded:

> Not even Arab intelligentsia are aware of developments
> in Israel in such fields as science, medicine, education,
> industry and agriculture. . . . Israelis, although better
> informed than their Arab neighbors, did not always per-
> ceive the important changes that had taken place in the
> Arab world since 1948. They spoke in stereotypes when
> it came to describing the Arab soldier, for example.
> They were not always aware of the Arab breakthrough
> in certain areas, such as the emancipation of women,
> growth in higher education, and improvement in agri-
> culture and industry. [From a manuscript made availa-
> ble to the author.]

While mutual misunderstanding is not necessarily due to lack of communication—insufficient motivation or ability to perceive one another correctly also may play a large role—the absence of direct contact appears to have been an important explanatory factor in this case. In 1956 Israel broke off talks in the Egyptian Mixed Armistice Commission, citing continuing attacks by fedayeen, and there followed a period of ten years of almost complete official noncommunication between Israel and the Arab nations. The Six-Day War in 1967 brought

121

renewed contacts, but of a military nature. Ambassador Gunnar Jarring, as special representative of the U.N. secretary-general, sought to reestablish official communication between the two sides after the war, but failed. Only rarely have there been Arab correspondents in Israel, or Israeli journalists in Arab states. The mass media on both sides have relied heavily on third party reports for information about the other. The two parties have communicated directly with each other through propaganda broadcasts, but the extent to which these one-way messages affected the thinking of either side is difficult to assess and is probably low.

As might be expected, the quality of Arab-Israeli communication—its ability to transmit meaning accurately—also has been low. Distortions in meaning have occurred not only in the transfer of information through third parties but also when the information transmitted was strained through a network of preconceptions. No matter what the message, the Arab tended to see only the Israeli who had taken some of his land and wanted more; the Israeli was likely to see only the Arab who wished to push him into the sea.

Lowering quality still further have been the differing styles of communication predominating in the two areas and the different connotations attached to the same words. The Arab practice has often been to make extreme statements that are not descriptive of subsequent, more moderate behavior. Israeli official statements usually have been judicious in tone but frequently followed by resolute action. When interviewed by James Reston in 1970, President Nasser of Egypt several times raised the question: What is peace? (New York Times, February 15, 1970). The question would not have had to raised if Nasser and Israeli leaders had shared a common definition.

Those in the Middle East who favored a compromise solution, or at least would have liked to make friendly gestures to the other side, have found little support from the mass media in the area. A Quaker group studying the situation in the late 1960s reported that both the Israeli and the Arab governments were increasingly wedded to a no-compromise line and to strident propaganda attacks on the other side. (American Friends Service Committee, 1970.) Arabs who advocated more moderate positions found it difficult to obtain a hearing in the mass media of the Arab states, and some even paid with their lives for their efforts at reconciliation. For example, Fawzi al-Husseini, a leading advocate of Arab cooperation with Jewish settlers, was assassinated in November 1946. King Abdullah of Jordan, who was regarded by many Arabs as a "collaborator" with the Israelis, was assassinated by a Palestinian in 1951. Arab residents of Israel have shown a marked reluctance to appear on Israeli television, even on nonpolitical and children's programs, although viewer mail has indicated that these programs are popular among the Arab population of Israel. (Katz, 1971.) Arab students abroad have reported strong pressure from organized Arab groups, and sometimes from their friends, to dissuade them from taking part with Israelis in any public discussion about the Middle East.

While pressures on Israelis have not been equally severe, they have been appreciable. Uri Avnieri, a self-proclaimed leader of what he called the "new forces" in Israel and a representative of a very small party in the Knesset, introduced a resolution advocating the creation of a Palestinian state immediately after the 1967 war. It was rejected by a vote of 188 to 2. Afterward, Avnieri reported, "twenty people within the government parties said they wanted to vote for it, but they had to vote the party line." (Stern, 1970.) Israelis who have spoken up in favor of compromise approaches have tended to be from among younger groups or those on the fringes of political life; they have rarely included members of the "establishment."

Partly as a result of the isolation of moderates on both sides— although Israeli moderates were somewhat less isolated—the mass media had the effect of reinforcing those who took rigid positions rather than preparing the ground for reconciliation. Israeli media gave full coverage to menacing statements by Arab spokesmen, while Arab media highlighted Israeli ambitions and intransigence. Premier Meir's formulation of the Israeli position as presented to the Knesset in December 1969 appeared to offer little basis for negotiation: "Between existence and non-existence there can be no compromise. Between life and extinction no formula can be found to enable a little of this and a little of that." Nor did Arab insistence that Israel agree in principle to return to its insecure pre-1967 boundaries before negotiation could start help to convince Israelis that conversations would be rewarding.

Much of the news and propaganda that reached the Middle East from other parts of the world also helped to reinforce rigid positions. American statements in support of Israel and Soviet statements promising aid in the redress of Arab grievances made compromise less necessary in the eyes of partisans on both sides. The United Nations, which one might have hoped would encourage voices of moderation, was instead used as a forum for contentious advocacy. Students of the Middle East have reported that Arab-Israeli coexistence was made even more difficult in areas on which foreign communications are focused, especially Jerusalem. Rather than serving as neutral third parties, most foreign spokesmen tended to become partisans and thereby to broaden the conflict.

THE ARAB-ISRAELI DIALOGUE AND THE ROLE OF
THIRD PARTIES

A wholesale restructuring of communication patterns in the Middle East in such a way that communication would make a larger contribution to a solution to the Arab-Israeli conflict is not likely. The major mass media will remain under pressure from governments and from their own audiences. Extreme and hostile statements will continue to make news. Political leaders and members of the public will still seek out and give their attention to communications that justify their ambitions and fears, hopes and grievances.

Nevertheless, investment of a modest amount of funds and energy by third parties, and possibly by some groups and individuals in the Middle East, might make possible a number of worthwhile changes. These efforts should seek to localize the dispute as much as possible, to open new channels of communication and to enrich existing ones, and to keep alive the vision of a settlement that would be acceptable— or even welcome—in the eyes of all parties concerned.

Localization of the conflict would involve the disengagement of outside powers and interest groups. Even if this should be politically possible, it would involve much more than communication—the instrument with which we are concerned here. However, within the framework of communication it is conceivable that some steps could be taken without involving changes in basic political positions. One avenue would be for the United States and the Soviet Union to explore the possibility of agreeing on certain principles to govern their respective propaganda activities in the Middle East. The two powers have previously talked about eliminating "war propaganda." These discussions have broken down because each side has a different communication system and a differing definition of propaganda, but an agreement with respect to a specified problem in a particular part of the world would seem more likely. Even if no agreement can be reached, discussion of the question could have a salutary influence in that both powers would then be on record as having agreed in principle that propaganda in the area should somehow be toned down.

A more ambitious and difficult step would be to seek an international agreement in the United Nations on the limitation of propaganda in the Middle East. Even a weak resolution of the General Assembly could be a positive influence if it called attention to the danger of inflammatory communications or provided guidelines for more constructive ones.

There is some risk in these initiatives. If either or both failed completely, they might call attention to outside involvement in the Middle East dispute and result in more rigid adherence to existing propaganda lines. Exploratory steps would have to weigh potential gains against potential losses.

Whether the particular measures suggested here are correct or not, one of the goals of those concerned with limiting the scope of the conflict should be to restrain outside propaganda involvement. Instead of serving as a focal point for divisive communications from all points of the compass, the Middle East should insofar as possible be transformed into a subject for sympathetic and concerned observation. Outside groups and powers would then more nearly play the role of third parties in a dispute. Their attention, rather than serving to embolden belligerents on both sides, would tend to become a restraining influence.

Another way third parties could help would be to provide additional neutral channels for communication between the Israeli and Arab groups directly involved. A few relatively neutral channels exist, such as those provided by the United Nations and a number of nonpartisan peace groups. But most available channels suffer from the suspicion with which they are viewed by one side or the other. This is especially true of mass media in the Arab states and in Israel. It is also true of official or semi-official media based in the United States or the Soviet Union. Of national voices, the BBC is probably the one that enjoys the greatest credibility throughout the Middle East, although many Israelis view it with suspicion.

Therefore, much of the burden for providing communication channels that are at least relatively trusted by both sides reverts to the United Nations and to private, nongovernmental groups. The United Nations, through its truce teams and negotiators at various levels, has performed yeoman service in bringing Israeli viewpoints to Arab governments and Arab viewpoints to the Israeli government. U.N. information centers, which maintain reference libraries and supply information about the United Nations to local media and scholars, serve all countries of the Middle East, even though not every country has such a center within its borders. Israel, Egypt, Syria, and Iraq all subscribe to international television news agency services that regularly distribute coverage of the United Nations.

U.N. information services are subjected to severe limiting factors. They suffer from underfinancing and understaffing; with more money and personnel they could extend their reach considerably. Since they serve an international organization, they cannot undertake activities or discuss subjects that would meet with substantial opposition by member governments. And, for the most part, they do not reach large numbers of people directly and have to rely mainly on national channels. Thus, while Israel relays the shortwave news program originated by the U.N. Office of Public Information, Egypt and Syria do not. Media in all countries of the area use some materials provided by the United Nations, but they also decide how to use them and what to include or exclude. (Information concerning

U.N. information activities is taken mainly from a report of the secretary-general entitled "Review and Reappraisal of United Nations Information Policies and Activities," A/C, 5/1320/Rev. 1, dated June 15, 1971.)

Of private communication channels, the international wire services are the most significant. A large proportion of current news about the Middle East reaches all parties through the facilities of these services. However, much of this news is rewritten by national news agencies or media before it reaches a mass audience. In addition, the individual media can choose what to present and what not to present. Ample opportunity is afforded for national biases to enter into news items based on the reporting of the international agencies.

Private radio has a better chance of reaching audiences in the Middle East directly. One such station started broadcasting regular programs early in 1973. It was the shipboard transmitter financed by Abie J. Nathan, an Israeli "peacenik" anchored in international waters between Haifa, Israel, and Port Said, Egypt. Programming consisted mainly of Arab and Israeli pop music, together with regular news bulletins. The station called itself the "Voice of Peace" and used the tune "Give Peace a Chance" as its musical signature. (New York Times, May 24, 1973.)

The extent to which the "Voice of Peace" was able to establish credibility and acceptance in the Middle East has not been determined. As far as Arab audiences are concerned, it had to contend with the fact that Nathan is an Israeli citizen, although his government did not support his activities. Israeli audiences, on the other hand, may have seen Nathan as a subversive influence. In any event, financial difficulties forced the station off the air before the end of 1973.

It would be highly desirable for nonpartisan groups to establish another such operation. The costs would not be large and the potential for encouraging dialogue would be great. Ideally, the groups concerned should consist of persons of good will from outside the Middle East who are not identified with either side. If they were willing to forego any particular formula for solving the Arab-Israeli dispute and to content themselves with providing a neutral channel through which those directly involved could search for such a formula, they could approximate the functions of a third party who offers "good offices" to ensure a continuing dialogue. Establishment of a propaganda channel by those with no ax to grind would in itself be a worthwhile innovation in international relations.

Person-to-person communication may also be helpful. Personal contacts among representatives of varying points of view can, cumulatively, affect large numbers of people. Such contacts also can have "pass-along" effects, as parties to each encounter talk to others or when discussions are reported by the news media.

A number of attempts have been made to provide neutral forums at which representatives and partisans of both Arab and Israeli points of view can meet and exchange ideas on neutral ground and in the presence of uncommitted observers. One such opportunity was offered by the Middle East Institute in Washington, D.C., which sponsored a conference in October 1970 on the theme "Violence and Dialogue in the Middle East." According to a conference report about, "positions on both sides converged to some degree in a consensus that Palestine must be viewed in a new light." (Stern, 1970.) An observer of the Middle East situation, while doubting that Americans could contribute very much to the active pursuit of peace in the area, has suggested that they could make an indirect contribution by providing channels of communication and exploring new alternatives. He concludes, "It cannot be said that anything serious has been done to realize these possibilities." (Chomsky, 1969, p. 17.) The provision of additional neutral forums for exchanges among those directly involved in the Middle East conflict is a promising opportunity.

Another kind of interpersonal contact cumulatively approximating mass communication was provided by Arabs who traveled between Israel and neighboring states. These consisted in part of Israeli residents who crossed into Arab states for personal or business reasons, and in part of Arab tourists who visited Israel for longer or shorter periods. During the summer of 1972 approximately 150,000 Arab tourists crossed Israeli border posts. While these travelers were not neutrals in the conflict, they nevertheless were in a position to carry large amounts of first-hand information between Israel and Arab countries, and to this extent contributed to more accurate knowledge on each side.

Tourism in general throughout the Middle East should be given more attention as a potentially massive communication channel. Some of it is stimulated for propaganda purposes, as when one country or another has imported visitors in order to impress them with its own point of view, but most tourism does not fall in this category. The question of what, specifically, could be done by tourists to promote a fruitful dialogue in the Middle East has never been asked, let alone answered. It should certainly receive consideration in the context of further inquiry devoted to determining what role communication might play in the advancement of peace.

Direct mail, like individual travel, is a species of point-to-point communication that in the aggregate may become a mass medium. It has been used extensively by partisans in the Middle East conflict, but has received much less attention from neutral parties promoting conciliation. An interesting possibility offered by direct mail is that, through its use, one could ensure that leaders in both Israel and the Arab states had at least the opportunity of exposing themselves to identical materials. A weekly newsletter mailed to a carefully selected list by a neutral private organization might not actually be read by all addressees, but it would provide one of the few possibilities of ensuring that at least some opinion leaders on both sides were giving their attention to the same questions, even though they were not discussing them directly with each other. Whether such a newsletter would be excluded from some nations by customs or postal authorities remains to be seen, but if it started on a modest scale and achieved a reputation for unswerving fairness it would be likely to get through.

SOME GOALS FOR MASS COMMUNICATION IN THE MIDDLE EAST

The objectives of peace-seeking communication in the Middle East could be substantially the same as those outlined more abstractly in the foregoing chapters. Of course some modifications would have to be introduced in view of the special characteristics of the area and situation. In general, communication between Israelis and Arabs should be maximized in quantity and quality; it should focus attention on problems and opportunities for solving them; it should help to mobilize groups and public opinion on both sides in favor of peaceful solutions; it should do as much as possible to prepare the ground for negotiation; and it should foster a mood in which peaceful solutions would be accepted.

Various measures for increasing the quantity of communication between Arabs and Israelis have already been suggested. These, for the most part, involve third parties. It is doubtful that an increase in the propaganda activities of governments and partisans on either side would have beneficial results, although this could be argued. One might reason that additional propaganda, no matter how inflammatory or tendentious, could not make the situation worse than it already is and might have the effect of making more information available. On the other hand, the dangers of merely reinforcing feelings of fear and hate appear to be considerable.

Efforts to improve the quality of communication should include steps to increase accuracy, to avoid stereotypes, and to put events and statements in context. In some cases it may be possible to encourage media under the direct or indirect control of governments or partisans to take measures along these lines. Even slight improvements, perhaps brought about through informal suggestions by U.N. personnel or third powers, would be significant. The quality of third party communications is especially important since these are more likely to gain acceptance by people on both sides of the dispute.

Accuracy is already a goal of most professional communicators. It is a quality that is held in especially high esteem by the international wire services. And even the most contentious propagandist does not relish being caught in a lie. Nevertheless, in a situation such as that in the Middle East, it is more difficult than in most areas to give a veridical picture of reality and to ensure that errors of fact do not creep into news dispatches or other forms of communication. As one student of the area put it, "there's just a tremendous amount of misinformation abroad in the world about the nature of the conflict and the nature of the points of view of the parties to that conflict." (Bolling, 1971, p. 54.)

There is no way even the most conscientious communicator can achieve complete accuracy, but it would appear that a special situation demands special measures. These might include greater care in checking facts, allocation of more time for preparing news stories or other materials, and extensive use of neutral experts.

A tendency to employ stereotypes is perhaps more common among nonprofessional communicators than among newsmen, but all of us resort to stereotypes on occasion. To quote a Quaker observer once more, "Many individuals have a tendency to speak in simplistic terms of 'the Arab position' or 'the Israeli position'. . . . This is all nonsense." (Bolling, 1971, p. 54.) Especially in a conflict situation, it is important to give full value to the different nuances of opinion on both sides and to avoid picturing large groups as though they were composed exclusively of one type of person. Stereotyping tends to obscure just those communalities of interests, characteristics, or values on which successful compromise and conciliation might be based.

Efforts to place statements and events in context have always been a mark of responsible journalism and sound scholarship, although both journalists and scholars often find this difficult. Particularly in the Middle East, the dramatic quality of inflammatory statements and shocking events is likely to overwhelm qualifications and efforts to achieve proportion. Threats made by political leaders and military forays by regular or irregular forces must be reported, but it can also be pointed out that the threats may be made largely for domestic consumption and that military action has failed to solve anything. Further, both statements and actions by those on one side of the dispute may on occasion be vigorously opposed by others on the same side. This, too, is part of the context.

The aim of improved quantity and quality in communication is to ensure that as much meaning as possible is transmitted from one party to another. Ideally, an Arab leader in Cairo should understand Israeli points of view as well as an editor in Tel Aviv, and the mayor of a city in Israel should know Arab approaches as well as an official in Damascus. The most elaborate communication system can only approximate such an ideal, and even with increased third party inputs, communication in the Middle East will still fall far short of maximum possible efficiency. Therefore those who control or influence the various media will have to make decisions as to what aspects of reality will be stressed.

One area that previous chapters have suggested for special attention is that of incipient conflict. That is, the media can make opinion leaders and policy-makers aware of problems that may cause even greater difficulties if they are not solved—the "early warning" function of communication.

It now seems anachronistic to speak of "early warning" in the Middle East, although with the benefit of hindsight one can identify points at which communication might have performed this function in the past. Most obviously, early Zionist leaders should have been induced to give more attention to the necessity of reaching an accommodation with the Arab population of Palestine. The misleading character of such slogans as "a land without people for a people without land" should have been pointed out more relentlessly. Following the U.N. Resolution on Palestine of 1947, greater attention should have been given to working out machinery for the enforcement of this resolution. Prior to the Six-Day War, the danger of demanding the withdrawal of U.N. observers should have been made clear to leaders in Arab countries as well as to the U.N. membership in general. Other particular times when communications could have played a role in calling attention to dangerous situations could doubtless be identified. Perhaps the war of October 1973 could not have been anticipated by the mass media, but third party communications could have stressed more heavily that any renewed conflict of this nature would be enormously costly to both sides.

Nor is it impossible that experts could even now identify critical problems that should be given more thought than they are receiving. The community of students of the Middle East—in Arab states, in Israel, and in third countries—comprises a rich infrastructure from which the media can draw. If the media can tap this infrastructure more systematically, they may be able to hasten the search for solutions to problems that, if neglected, could become worse.

A related function of the mass media is to call attention to opportunities. In addition to helping to forestall deterioration, the media might be able to hasten improvements in Arab-Israeli relations. At first, these improvements probably would be of a minor character: For example, by pointing out parallelism of interests in regard to the holy places, where some cooperation has previously existed, it might be possible to devise arrangements that would be more satisfactory to both sides. Similarly, there may be limited economic objectives that are shared by Arabs and Israelis. Working out an equitable sharing of water resources may be a case in point. By focusing on such opportunities, the mass media can help to ensure that they are fully explored and are not quietly sabotaged by those who would prefer to see the situation deteriorate.

Perhaps the most important contribution that mass communication could make toward resolution of the Arab-Israeli conflict would be to strengthen and encourage those on both sides who are seeking peaceful solutions, to help them recruit more adherents to their points of view, to put them in touch with each other, and to foster the organization of public opinion favoring peaceful solutions.

There appears to be agreement among students of the Middle East that there is great diversity of opinion among both Arabs and Israelis about what political course their respective governments should steer. (American Friends Service Committee, 1970; Halpern, 1972; Kadduri, 1969; Rubinstein, 1970.) Some are more in favor of conciliation and peaceful solutions than others. Yet on the Arab side there is great pressure on moderates to keep their views to themselves. They tend to feel isolated and powerless. There is little communication among them. They do not have access to communication channels used by Arab governments and hard-line partisans of the Arab cause.

Pressures on Israeli moderates have not been as great. Their voices have been audible, and they have been aware of each other. Nevertheless, they have been subjected to more subtle discouragement, in the form of ridicule, snubs by members of the "establishment," and even charges that they lack patriotism. Some observers have suggested that the October war of 1973 had the effect of driving many of them into the ranks of the "hard-liners." (Rubinstein, 1973).

A major task of third party communications is to seek out moderates on both sides, to offer them channels and forums, and to confer on them the standing and prestige that is a byproduct of respectful attention by the mass media. Those actively seeking peaceful solutions could be made aware that they are not alone; those who have been passive and discouraged could be activated; a few of those who have been disinterested might be won over. Third party radios and publications might experiment with "letters to the editor" columns. The identities of some correspondents might have to be protected, but this is customary under some other conditions too. In effect, these media could serve as "house organs" for those desirous of finding peaceful solutions to the Middle East conflict. It is possible that this mode of communication among like-minded individuals would lead to direct contacts among them and to the formation of organizations.

To the extent that public opinion or formal organizations devoted to a search for nonviolent solutions did take shape, the opportunities for negotiation among governments would be improved. Even relatively weak organizations of this nature, or a minority public opinion, would make governments less captives of hard-liners in their own countries. In the case of the Palestinians, who have no government to speak for them, current leaders would feel somewhat freer to speak in tones of moderation and the emergence of more moderate leaders would be facilitated.

Communication can help prepare the ground for negotiation, direct or indirect, in other ways as well. It can help acquaint both sides with as many alternatives as possible—in effect providing a generous menu from which specifics might be selected by interested parties. It can describe to each side the problems and grievances of the other, emphasizing that the other side is unlikely to find any solution to be easy or without cost. It can confer recognition on spokesmen for both sides who favor negotiation or other forms of conflict resolution. This could be done by quoting back to the Middle East the favorable reactions of leaders of other countries, or in other ways. A goal of all these measures would be to make negotiation a familiar, reasonable, and nonthreatening concept, one that can be readily accepted.

One way that third parties might broaden the range of alternatives under discussion and encourage negotiation would be to arrange a series of political games. These simulations would make it possible to explore the implications of moves toward the relaxation of tension that either side might now find too risky to take. For instance, one could gain insights into the kinds of effects that might follow a very generous Israeli offer or a magnanimous Arab proposal. If such games were expertly conducted, and if synopses of them could be televised or published in booklet form, they would be likely to interest elite audiences on both sides of the conflict—and possibly would attract a mass audience as well.

Or a number of small group discussions along the lines of those conducted by Doob or Burton could be sponsored by third parties. (Doob, 1969; Burton, 1969.) These could involve either Middle Eastern experts from outside the area who would be assigned Arab or Israeli roles or, preferably, Israeli and Arab students of foreign policy. Summaries of these discussions, disseminated by broadcast or print media, would be likely to achieve widespread attention. The identifies of the participants might have to be withheld in some cases.

While providing information that might help to bring about negotiation, or to assist the process when it occurs, communication also can encourage a mood favorable to conflict resolution in general. Presenting each side in human terms, rather than in stereotypes, is likely to help in any dispute. Emphasis on what unites the contending parties rather than on what divides them is another general rule.

The axiom that there is a solution both sides would prefer to warfare applies to almost all conflict situations.

It is for those who are thoroughly familiar with the Middle East to suggest the themes that would be most likely to lead to a mood conducive to peace in that area. One possibility would be to emphasize the values traditionally associated with both cultures: the Arab's generosity, the Jew's love of justice, the respect of each for learning. A related approach would be to draw on religious scriptures—the Koran, the Bible, and others—and remind audiences in the area of the passages that counsel reconciliation. The scriptures have been used extensively by those promoting nationalistic viewpoints, and it would be appropriate to enlist them in the struggle for international understanding.

Another approach would be to place the present in the broad sweep of history, picturing the constantly changing patterns in the Middle East and treating the current state of affairs as one detail in a long tapestry. A third party voice would be able to say: We expect more from two of the most innovative peoples in history than the perpetuation of territorial disputes. We do not know what the solution should be, but those who have brought forth two of the world's great religions can certainly find ways to adjust their differences.

There are many possibilities. Their purpose would be to suggest values and interpretations that go beyond the slogans justifying conflict and to help provide an intellectual and emotional base for those who are predisposed toward peaceful solutions.

A POSTSCRIPT

This discussion has been predicated on the assumption that a stable peace in the Middle East can be brought about only by those who are directly involved: primarily the Israelis, the Palestinians, and the Arab states. The role of communication has been seen as that of helping to create conditions under which these parties can find solutions acceptable to all. Communication is being pressed into service to serve somewhat the same functions as a mediator in a dispute. The mediator may provide neutral ground on which to meet, he may carry messages from one side to another, and he may suggest possible lines of action. But he is not committed to any particular solution. The correct solution must be identified and accepted by the parties themselves.

Perhaps such an approach is unrealistic. There are those who maintain that the key to peace in the Middle East is to be found not in the area itself but in Washington and Moscow. If this is indeed the case, then communication would have a different role to play. However, it seems reasonable to assume that, even if all outside powers were to become disinterested, an ample number of problems would remain to be solved. Their solution might be somewhat easier, but this solution would still have to be found by those directly involved.

At the same time, the foregoing discussion may undervalue the potential role of mass media currently based in Arab states and in Israel. Perhaps these media could do more than third party media to bridge the differences of the contending parties and find a formula for constructive cooperation among all the peoples of the Middle East. Indeed, perhaps the intervention of third parties would do more harm than good although, again, this does not seem likely.

Whatever the role of the mass media in bringing peace to the Middle East, one must assume that communication has a role. It is an element that enters into all human relationships; furthermore, it is relatively inexpensive and highly malleable in the hands of man. If the role suggested here is not the correct one, then the significance of this discussion is only to call attention to the desirability of determining the proper role and how to bring it about—not only in the Middle East but in all areas where the threat of international conflict exists.

Communication in domestic political processes has been extensively studied and even more extensively used. The same is true with respect to communication in warfare. Communication is employed with considerable precision to promote sales, and with less precision but great effect to promote ideologies. Yet our understanding of how to use this instrument in the reconciliation of peoples with different interests and different ideologies has lagged. As our planet grows smaller almost daily, it becomes ever more urgent to close this knowledge gap.

Abu Bakr, Yehya. "The Use and Abuse of Semantics in Mass Communication," in Mass Media and International Understanding. Ljubljana, Yugoslavia: School of Sociology, Political Science and Journalism, University of Ljubljana, 1969.

Academy for Educational Development, New York. "Observations on International Negotiations." June 1971 (mimeo.).

_____. Report on International Education 1, no. 1 (December 1972).

Acheson, Dean. Present at the Creation. New York: New American Library, 1969.

Alexander, Yonah. The Role of Communication in the Middle East Conflict: Ideological and Religious Aspects. New York: Praeger Publishers, 1974.

Almond, Gabriel A. The American People and Foreign Policy. New York: Praeger Publishers, 1960.

American Assembly. "Japanese-American Relations III." New York: Columbia University, 1972.

American Friends Service Committee. Search for Peace in the Middle East. Philadelphia: the Committee, 1970.

Angell, Robert C. Peace on the March: Transnational Participation. New York: Van Nostrand Reinhold, 1969.

ANPA News Research Bulletin, no. 9 (June 3, 1970).

Appelbaum, Stephen A. "The World in Need of a 'Leader': An Application of Group Psychology of International Relations," British Journal of Medical Psychology 40 (December 1967).

Aronson, James. Deadline for the Media. Indianapolis: Bobbs-Merrill, 1972.

Bagdikian, Ben. The Effete Conspiracy and Other Crimes by the Press. New York: Harper and Row, 1972.

Bailey, Sydney D. Peaceful Settlement of Disputes: Ideas and Proposals for Research. New York: UNITAR, 1971.

Ball, George W. "Slogans and Realities," Foreign Affairs 47, no. 4 (July 1969).

Bernays, Edward L. Address before the joint annual meeting of the Association of Canadian Advertisers and the Advertising and Sales Club of Toronto, Toronto, October 28, 1943 (mimeo.).

Bloomfield, Lincoln P. "Peacekeeping and Peacemaking," Foreign Affairs 44, no. 4 (July 1966).

Bogart, Leo. "Warning: The Surgeon General Has Determined that TV Violence Is Moderately Dangerous to Your Child's Mental Health," Public Opinion Quarterly 36, no. 4 (winter 1972-73).

Bolling, Landrum R. In "Observations on International Negotiations." New York: Academy for Educational Development, June 1971 (transcript of an informal conference).

Bonham, G. Matthew. "Simulating International Disarmament Negotiations," Journal of Conflict Resolution 15, no. 3 (September 1971).

Brown, Robert U. "Shop Talk at Thirty," Editor and Publisher, June 6, 1970.

Brzezinski, Zbigniew. "The Framework of East-West Reconciliation," Foreign Affairs 46, no. 2 (January 1968).

_____. "How the Cold War Was Played," Foreign Affairs 51, no. 1 (October 1972).

Buchanan, Patrick J. Letter to New York Times, January 8, 1971.

Buchanan, William, and Hadley Cantril. How Nations See Each Other. Urbana: University of Illinois Press, 1953.

Burton, John W. Conflict and Communication: The Use of Controlled Communication in International Relations. New York: Free Press, 1969.

Caplow, Theodore, and Kurt Finsterbusch. "France and Other Countries: A Study of International Interaction," Journal of Conflict Resolution 12, no. 1 (March, 1968).

Carnegie Endowment for International Peace. "Some Aspects of Mediation." Report of a conference sponsored by the European Center of the Carnegie Endowment for International Peace, Talloires, France, June 1969.

Chomsky, Noam. "Nationalism and Conflict in Palestine," Columbia Forum 12, no. 4 (winter 1969).

Cleveland, Harlan; Gerard J. Mangone; and John C. Adams. The Overseas Americans. New York: McGraw-Hill, 1960.

Coddington, Alan. "Policies Advocated in Conflict Situations by British Newspapers," Journal of Peace Research, no. 4 (1965).

Cohen, Bernard C. "The Present and the Press," World Politics 13, no. 1 (October 1960).

_____. The Press and Foreign Policy. Princeton, N. J.: Princeton University Press, 1963.

Coleman, James S. Community Conflict. New York: Free Press, 1957.

Committee on Foreign Affairs, U.S. House of Representatives. "A Congressional Look at the U.N." Subcommittee report presented in Vista, January-February 1971.

Cronkite, Walter. "The Journalist at Thermopolae." William Allen White lecture, University of Kansas, 1969.

Danielson, Wayne A., and G. C. Wilhoit, Jr. A Computerized Bibliography of Mass Communication Research, 1944-64. New York: Magazine Publishers Association, 1967.

d'Arcy, Jean. "Challenge to Cooperation," Saturday Review, October 24, 1970.

Davison, W. Phillips. "Communication Channels Since World War II," in Harold D. Lasswell, Daniel Lerner, and Hans Speier, eds., Communication and Propaganda in World History, Vol. III. Cambridge, Mass.: MIT Press, forthcoming.

_____. "Communication on Vietnam: A Utopian Perpsective." Paper presented at the meeting of the American Psychological Association, New York, September 2, 1966.

_____. International Political Communication. New York: Praeger Publishers, 1965.

_____. "International and World Public Opinion," in Ithiel de Sola Pool, Wilbur Schramm et al., eds., Communication Handbook. Chicago: Rand McNally, 1973.

_____. "Making Sense of Vietnam News," Columbia Journalism Review 5, no. 4 (Winter 1966-67).

Dean, Arthur S. Test Ban and Disarmament: The Path of Negotiations. New York: Harper and Row, 1966.

Deutsch, Karl W. "Mass Communications and the Loss of Freedom in National Decision-Making: A Possible Research Approach to Interstate Conflict," Journal of Conflict Resolution 1, no. 2 (1957).

Diamond, Edwin. "How the White House Keeps Its Eye on the Network News Shows," New York Magazine, May 10, 1971.

Donovan, Thomas A. "Political Reporting Trends," Foreign Service Journal, November 1963.

Doob, Leonard W.; William J. Foltz; and Robert B. Stevens. "The Fermeda Workshop: A Different Approach to Border Conflicts in East Africa," Journal of Psychology 73 (1969).

Dougherty, Philip H. "Advertising: Challenging Products' Claims," New York Times, April 29, 1971.

Dulles, Allan. "The Craft of Intelligence," Harper's Magazine, April 1963.

Dunn, Frederick S. War and the Minds of Men. New York: Harper, 1950.

Eckhardt, William, and Ralph K. White. "A Test of the Mirror-Image Hypothesis: Kennedy and Khrushchev," Journal of Conflict Resolution 11, no. 3 (September 1967).

Edmead, Frank. "Analysis and Prediction in International Mediation." New York: UNITAR, 1971.

Erskine, Hazel. "The Polls: Pollution and Its Costs," Public Opinion Quarterly 36, no. 1 (spring 1972).

Evan, William. "Transnational Forums," in Quincy Wright, William
    Evan, and Mortimer Deutsch, eds., Preventing World War III.
    New York: Simon and Schuster, 1962.

Fisher, Glen H. Public Diplomacy and the Behavioral Sciences.
    Bloomington: University of Indiana Press, 1972.

Fisher, Roger. International Conflict for Beginners. New York:
    Harper and Row, 1969.

Forsberg, R. Appendix in Gould, L. N.

Frank, Jerome D. Sanity and Survival. New York: Vintage Books,
    1968.

Free, Lloyd A., and Hadley Cantril. The Political Beliefs of Americans.
    New Brunswick, N. J.: Rutgers University Press, 1967.

Friedrich, Carl J. Europe: An Emergent Nation. New York: Harper
    and Row, 1969.

Galbraith, J. Kenneth. "Making Foreign Policy: The Influence of Men
    and Events," Current, December 1969.

Galtung, Johan. "East-West Interaction Patterns," Journal of Peace
    Research, no. 2 (1966).

_____. "International TV Panels in Times of Crisis," Bulletin of
    Peace Proposals, no. 1 (1970).

_____. "Peace," in International Encyclopedia of the Social Sciences,
    Vol. 11. New York: Macmillan and Free Press, 1968.

_____ and Mari H. Ruge. "The Structure of Foreign News," Journal
    of Peace Research, no. 1 (1965).

Gardner, Richard N. "Space Communications—A New Instrument for
    World Peace." Paper presented at the Columbia Scholastic
    Press Association annual conference, March 15, 1969.

George, Alexander L. Propaganda Analysis. Evanston, Ill.: Row,
    Peterson, 1959.

Glenn, Edmund S. "Semantic Difficulties in International Communica-
    tion," Etc. 11, no. 3 (1954).

_____, et al. "A Cognitive Inter-Active Model to Analyze Culture in International Relations," Journal of Conflict Resolution 14, no. 1 (March 1970).

Goldhamer, Herbert, and Hans Speier. "Some Observations on Political Gaming," World Politics, October 1959.

Gordenker, Leon. The U.N. Secretary General and the Maintenance of Peace. New York: Columbia University Press, 1967.

Gould, Loyal N. The ENDC and the Press. Stockholm: Swedish International Peach Research Institute, 1969.

Gould, Wesley L. "'The New York Times' and the Development of Assurance Between Adversary Nations: Six Case Studies, 1961-63," Technical Report 2 in the series, Social and Psychological Aspects of Verification, Inspection and International Assurance. Prepared for the U.S. Arms Control and Disarmament Agency, by the Purdue Research Foundation, Purdue University, West Lafayette, Indiana, December 1968 (mimeo.).

Graber, Doris. "The Press as Opinion Resource During the 1968 Presidential Campaign," Public Opinion Quarterly 35, no. 2 (summer 1971).

Granitsas, Spyridon. "On U.N.'s 25th Birthday—Whole World Isn't Tuned In," Editor and Publisher, October 24, 1970.

Halpern, Manfred. Review of Arab Attitudes Toward Israel by Yehoshafat Harkabi, in Saturday Review, June 10, 1972.

Hamilton, Richard F. "A Research Note on the Mass Support for 'Tough' Military Initiative," American Sociological Review 33, no. 3 (June 1968).

Hohenberg, John. The Professional Journalist. New York: Holt, Rinehart and Winston, 1969.

Holsti, Karl J. "Resolving International Conflicts: A Taxonomy of Behavior and Some Figures on Procedures," Journal of Conflict Resolution 10, no. 3 (September 1966).

Holsti, Ole. R. "The 1914 Case," American Political Science Review 59, no. 2 (1965).

Holton, Thomas. "Peace in Vietnam Through Due Process: An Unexplored Path," American Bar Association Journal 54, no. 1 (January 1968).

Iklé, Fred C. Every War Must End. New York: Columbia University Press, 1971.

International Broadcast Institute. "Report of the Second Conference on Aspects of Television News Coverage," Grottaferrata, Italy, March 1970.

_____. IBI Newsletter, autumn 1970.

Jack, Homer A. "Confrontation in Stockholm," War/Peace Report 7 (August-September 1967).

Jervis, Robert. The Logic of Images in International Relations. Princeton, N.J.: Princeton University Press, 1970.

Johnson, Lyndon B. The Vantage Point: Perspectives of the Presidency, 1963-1969. New York: Holt, Rinehart and Winston, 1971.

Kadduri, Majdia, ed. The Arab-Israeli Impasse: Expressions of Moderate Viewpoints . . . by Well-Known Western Writers. Washington, D.C.: R. B. Luce, 1969.

Katz, Elihu. "Television Comes to the Middle East," Trans-Action 8, no. 8 (June 1971).

Kelman, Herbert C. "The Problem-Solving Workshop in Conflict Resolution," in Richard L. Merritt, ed., Communication in International Politics. Urbana: University of Illinois Press, 1972.

Klapper, Joseph T. The Effects of Mass Communication. Glencoe, Ill.: Free Press, 1960.

Kolosov, Y. M. "The Law and Scientific and Technical Progress: Mass Information and International Law," Sovetskoye Gesudarstvo i Pravo, no. 11 (November 1972). In Current Digest of the Soviet Press 23, no. 14 (April 11, 1973).

_____. "The Mass Media and International Law," International Affairs (Moscow), July 1973.

Kraft, Joseph. "The Future of the New York Times." Esquire, April 1961.

Kruglak, Theodore E. "The Foreign Correspondents," Nieman Reports, January 1957.

Kurtz, Howard G., and Harriet B. Kurtz. "The Collapse of U.S. Global Strategy," U.S. Command and General Staff College Military Review, May 1969.

Lambert, Richard D. "Language and Area Study Review," Items (Social Science Research Council, New York) 27, no. 2 (June 1973).

Larock, Victor. "The United Nations and the Armaments Race," Review of International Affairs 21 (June 5, 1970).

Larsen, Otto N. "Social Effects of Mass Communication," in Robert E. L. Faris, ed., Handbook of Modern Sociology. Chicago: Rand McNally, 1964.

Lasswell, Harold D. Propaganda Technique in the World War. New York: Knopf, 1927.

Latey, Maurice. "Broadcasting to Eastern Europe," Survey, summer 1973.

Lazarsfeld, Paul F., and Robert K. Merton. "Mass Communications, Popular Taste, and Organized Social Action," in Lyman Bryson, ed., The Communication of Ideas. New York: Harper, 1948.

Leontiev, Lev A. "Über die Konvergenztheorie," Sowjetunion Heute 13 (September 1, 1968).

Lerner, Daniel. The Passing of Traditional Society. Glencoe, Ill.: Free Press, 1958.

Lewis, Sulwyn. "Principles of Cultural Cooperation," Reports and Papers on Mass Communication #61. Paris: UNESCO, 1970.

Lippitt, Ronald. "Sensitivity Training: The Here and Now of Experience," ISR Newsletter (University of Michigan), spring 1970.

Lippmann, Walter. Public Opinion. New York: Macmillan, 1922.

Loomis, Henry L., deputy director of USIA. Testimony before the Subcommittee on State Department Organization and Foreign Operations, Committee on Foreign Affairs, House of Representatives, USIA World, December 1971.

Loomis, J. L. "Communication, the Development of Trust and Cooperative Behavior," Human Relations 12, no. 4 (1959).

Mankekar, Dinker Rao. "Mass Media and International Understanding as a Newly-Emerged, Underdeveloped Country Looks at the Problem," in Mass Media and International Understanding, Ljubljana, Yugoslavia: School of Sociology, Political Science and Journalism, University of Ljubljana, 1969.

Marjanovic, Stevan, and Dimitrije Pindic. "Legal Position and Function of United Nations Information Centers," in Mass Media and International Understanding. Ljubljana, Yugoslavia: School of Sociology, Political Science and Journalism, University of Ljubljana, 1969.

Markham, James W. "Communication Research in International Conflict and Cooperation." Unpublished paper (prepared at the University of Iowa) cited in N. Bhaskara Rao, 1972.

Martin, L. John. International Propaganda: Its Legal and Diplomatic Control. Minneapolis: University of Minnesota Press, 1958.

Mass Media and International Understanding. Ljubljana, Yugoslavia: School of Sociology, Political Science and Journalism, University of Ljubljana, 1969.

Modelski, George. "The World's Foreign Ministers: A Political Elite," Journal of Conflict Resolution 14, no. 2 (June 1970).

Murray, Barbara E., and Morton Deutsch. "The Effects of Role Reversal During the Discussion of Opposing Viewpoints," Journal of Conflict Resolution 12, no. 3 (September 1968).

Najman, Velizar. "International Intercourse in the Light of Coherence of Information Freedom with National Security Protection," in Mass Media and International Understanding. Ljubljana, Yugoslavia: School of Sociology, Political Science and Journalism, University of Ljubljana, 1969.

Nemzer, Louis. "The Soviet Friendship Societies," Public Opinion Quarterly 13, no. 2 (summer 1949).

Olson, Theodore, and Gordon Christiansen. The Grindstone Experiment: Thirty-One Hours Toronto: Canadian Friends Service Committee, 1966.

Osgood, Charles E. An Alternative to War or Surrender. Urbana: University of Illinois Press, 1962.

Osolnik, Bogdan. "Some Problems Concerning International Communication," in Mass Media and International Understanding. Ljubljana, Yugoslavia: School of Sociology, Political Science and Journalism, University of Ljubljana, 1969.

Ostgaard, Einar. "Factors Influencing the Flow of News," Journal of Peace Research, no. 1 (1965).

Popovic, Milo. "About Some Features of Institutional and Non-Institutional Factors in International Communication," in Mass Media and International Understanding. Ljubljana, Yugoslavia: School of Sociology, Political Science and Journalism, University of Ljubljana, 1969.

Rao, N. Bhaskara. Indo-Pak Conflict: Controlled Mass Communication in Interstate Relations. New Delhi: S. Chand, 1972.

Rapoport, Anatol. Fights, Games and Debates. Ann Arbor: University of Michigan Press, 1960.

_____. Games Which Simulate Deterrence and Disarmament. Clarkson, Ont.: Canadian Peace Research Institute, 1967.

_____. Strategy and Conscience. New York: Harper and Row, 1964.

Reston, James. "The Number One Voice," In Lester Markel et al., Public Opinion and Foreign Policy. New York: Harper, 1949.

_____. "The Pentagon Battle Over Money and Strategy," New York Times, August 22, 1969.

Rich, Alexander. "Science and Survival: The Pugwash Conference at Sochi, U.S.S.R.," Science 166 (December 12, 1969).

Roshco, Bernard. "Making the Incredible Credible." Columbia Journalism Review 7, no. 2 (summer 1968).

_____. "The Phony Issue of News Management," Interplay, April 1970.

Rubinsteinm Amnon. "The Israelis: No More Doves," New York Times Magazine, October 21, 1973.

_____. "And Now in Israel a Fluttering of Doves," New York Times Magazine, July 26, 1970.

Russett, Bruce M., and W. Curtis Lamb. "Global Patterns of Diplomatic Exchange," Journal of Peace Research, no. 1 (1969).

Schieder, Theodor. "Friedenssicherung und Staatenpluralismus," Europa Archiv 24 (December 25, 1968).

Schiller, Herbert I. "International Communications, National Sovereignty and Domestic Insurgency," in Mass Media and International Understanding. Ljubljana, Yugoslavia: School of Sociology, Political Science and Journalism, University of Ljubljana, 1969.

Schramm, Wilbur. Mass Media and National Development. Stanford, Calif.: Stanford University Press; Paris: UNESCO, 1964.

Shure, Gerald H.; R. J. Meeker; and E. A. Hansford. "The Effectiveness of Pacifist Strategies in Bargaining Games," Journal of Conflict Resolution 9, no. 1 (March 1965).

Singer, Benjamin D. "Violence, Protest, and War in Television News: The U.S. and Canada Compared," Public Opinion Quarterly 34, no. 4 (winter 1970-71).

Singer, J. David. "Disarmament," in International Encyclopedia of the Social Sciences, Vol. 4. New York: Macmillan and Free Press, 1968.

Sington, Derrick, and Arthur Weidenfeld. The Goebbels Experiment. New Haven: Yale University Press, 1948.

Small, William. To Kill a Messenger. New York: Hastings House, 1970.

Smith, Don D. "Some Effects of Radio Moscow's North American Broadcasts," Public Opinion Quarterly 34, no. 4 (winter 1970-71).

Smythe, Dallas W. "Conflict, Cooperation and Communications Satellites," in Mass Media and International Understanding. Ljubljana,

Yugoslavia: School of Sociology, Political Science and Journalism, University of Ljubljana, 1969.

Solzhenitsyn, Alexandr. Excerpts from Nobel Prize Lecture, New York Times, August 25, 1972.

Speier, Hans. "Limited Peace," Orbis 12, no. 4 (winter 1969).

Stagner, Ross. Psychological Aspects of International Conflict. Belmont, Calif.: Brooks/Cole, 1967.

Stanley Foundation. "Fourth Conference on the United Nations of the Next Decade," Quebec, June 1969.

_____. "Report of the Third News Media Seminar at the United Nations," New York, December 1-3, 1971, Muscatine, Iowa, 1972.

_____. "Tenth Anniversary Strategy for Peace Conference Report," Muscatine, Iowa, 1970.

Stern, Paula. "Report" to the Alicia Patterson Fund. New York, October 1970 (mimeo.).

Stone, Jeremy S. Strategic Persuasion: Arms Limitation Through Dialogue. New York: Columbia University Press, 1967.

Strickland, Donald A. "Content Analysis." Technical Report 3 in the series, Social and Psychological Aspects of Verification, Inspection and International Assurance. Prepared for the U.S. Arms Control and Disarmament Agency by the Purdue Research Foundation, Purdue University, West Lafayette, Indiana, December 1968 (mimeo.).

Sullivan, Walter. "Kapitsa for U.S.-Soviet Convergence," New York Times, October 9, 1969.

Takeshi, Ishida. "Beyond the Traditional Concepts of Peace in Different Cultures," Journal of Peace Research, no. 2 (1969).

Taylor, George E., and Ben Cashman. The New United Nations: A Reappraisal of United States Policies. Washington, D.C.: American Enterprise Institute, 1965.

Tebbel, John. "Studying the Mass Media," Saturday Review, February 14, 1970.

United Nations. "Review and Reappraisal of United Nations Information
Policies and Activities: Report of the Secretary-General."
New York, A/C.5/1320/Rev. 1, June 15, 1971.

_____. "Review and Reappraisal of United Nations Information
Policies and Activities: Report of the Secretary-General."
New York, A/C.5/1452, October 17, 1972.

United Nations Association—U.S.A. "Space Communications: Increasing U.N. Responsiveness to the Problems of Mankind." New
York: UNA-USA, 1971a.

_____. "The United Nations in the 1970's." New York: UNA-USA,
1971b.

_____. "World Population: A Challenge to the United Nations and
Its System of Agencies." New York: UNA-USA, 1969.

United States Advisory Commission on Information. Twenty-fourth
Report to Congress, May 1969.

United States Information Agency. The Agency in Brief. Washington,
D.C., 1969.

U.S.I.A. World 5, no. 9 (April 1972). Letter from President Nixon
to Frank Shakespeare, director, United States Information Agency.

Van Dyke, Vernon. Human Rights, The United States, and World Community. New York: Oxford University Press, 1970.

Vreg, France. "Structural and Functional Changes in the Public and
the World Community," in Mass Media and International Understanding. Ljubljana, Yugoslavia: School of Sociology, Political
Science and Journalism, University of Ljubljana, 1969.

Walker, Charles G. Peacekeeping: 1969. Philadelphia: Friends
Peace Committee, 1969.

Walton, Richard E. "Conflict Management in Interagency Projects"
(Special Technical Report 3). Cambridge, Mass.: Graduate
School of Business Administration, Harvard University, June
1969 (mimeo.).

_____. "Interpersonal Confrontation and Basic Third Party Func-
tions: A Case Study," Journal of Applied Behavioral Science
4, no. 3 (1968).

_____. "A System of Attitudes Related to International Assurance: Theoretical Framework and Review." Technical Report 1 in the series, Social and Psychological Aspects of Verification, Inspection and International Assurance. Prepared for the U.S. Arms Control and Disarmament Agency by the Purdue Research Foundation, Purdue University, West Lafayette, Indiana. September 1968 (mimeo.).

_____ and John M. Dutton. "The Management of Interdepartmental Conflict: A Model and Review," Administrative Science Quarterly 14, no. 1 (March 1969).

_____; Wesley L. Gould; Donald A. Strickland; and Michael J. Driver. Social and Psychological Aspects of Verification, Inspection and International Assurance. Final Report Prepared for U.S. Arms Control and Disarmament Agency by Purdue Research Foundation, Purdue University, West Lafayette, Indiana. January 1969.

Washburn, A. Michael. "Peace Education is Alive—But Unsure of Itself," War/Peace Report, November 1971.

Watts, William, and Lloyd A. Free. State of the Nation. New York: Universe Books, 1973.

Weiss, Walter. "Effects of the Mass Media of Communication," in Gardner Lindzey and Elliot Aronson, eds., Handbook of Social Psychology, Vol. 5. 2nd ed.; Reading, Mass.: Addison-Wesley, 1968.

Welch, Susan. "The American Press and Indochina," in Richard L. Merritt, ed., Communication in International Politics. Urbana: University of Illinois Press, 1972.

Werkheiser, Don. "Invisible Tyranny: Symbolization in Human Relations, I" and "Invisible Tyranny: Toward the Alternative of Mutual Convenience, II," Journal of Human Relations 16, nos. 1 and 2, (1968 a and b).

White, Ralph K. "The New Resistance to International Propaganda," Public Opinion Quarterly 16, no. 4 (winter 1952-53).

_____. "'Socialism' and 'Capitalism,' An International Misunderstanding," Foreign Affairs 44, no. 2 (January 1966).

_____. "The Strategy of Communist and Non-Communist Communication with the Developing Countries," in Interkulturelle

Kommunikation Zwischen Industrielaender und Entwicklungslaen-
der. Berlin: Deutsches Institut fur Entwicklungspolitik, 1967.

_____. "Three Not-So-Obvious Contributions of Psychology to
Peace," Journal of Social Issues 25, no. 4 (1969).

White House Conference on International Cooperation. "Report of the
Committee on Arms Control and Disarmament," Washington,
D.C. November 28-December 1, 1965.

Whiting, Alan S. China Crosses the Yalu. New York: Macmillan, 1960.

Whyte, William H., Jr. Is Anybody Listening? New York: Simon and
Schuster, 1952.

Wright, Quincy. "The Study of War," in International Encyclopedia of
the Social Sciences, Vol. 16. New York: Macmillan and Free
Press, 1968.

York, Herbert. Race to Oblivion: A Participant's View of the Arms
Race, New York: Simon and Schuster, 1970.

Yu, Frederick T. C. Unpublished survey of foreign news in the American press, Columbia University Graduate School of Journalism,
1963.

Zajonc, Robert, "Brainwash: Familiarity Breeds Comfort," Psychology
Today 3, no. 9 (February 1970).

Gallup poll, 20, 21, 22
Galtung, Johan, 32, 48, 54, 67
games and simulations, 77-78,
  78-81
Gardner, Richard N., 111
gatekeeping in the media, 59
George, Alexander L., 91
Germany, 10, 86
Glenn, Edmund S., 36, 39
Goldhamer, Herbert, 79
Gordenker, Leon, 113
Gould, Loyal N., 59, 65, 92
Gould, Wesley L., 56, 98,
  102
Graber, Doris, 68
Granitas, Spyridon, 109
Grose, Peter, 121

Hambro, Edward, 39
Hamilton, Richard F., 58
Hansford, E. A., 98
Harkabi, Yehoshafat, 131
Harris poll, 20, 23
Helsinki Conference (see Conference
  on European Security and Co-
  operation)
Hohenberg, John, 54, 58, 64
Holsti, Karl J., 41
Holsti, Ole R., 28
Holton, Thomas, 41

Iklé, Fred C., 40, 42
India, 42
intelligence reports, 17, 39, 85
International Broadcast Institute,
  38, 68
international communication; quality
  of, 34ff, 59ff, 90ff, 110-112;
  quantity of, 26ff, 53-54, 59ff,
  110-111; two-way, 32-33, 34-35,
  59-60, 66, 76, 88-89
International Court of Justice, 43
International Peace Research
  Institute, Oslo, 4
International Press Institute, 34

intra-organizational conflict, 27-28,
  72
Iraq, 125
Israel, 19, 22, 125 (see also Middle
  East)

Jack, Homer A., 49
Japan, 29, 76
Japan Broadcasting Corporation,
  68
Japan Foundation, 76
Japanese-American Assembly,
  29, 76
Jarring, Gunnar, 122
Jervis, Robert, 83, 98
Johnson, Lyndon B., 16, 17, 20, 21
Journal of Conflict Resolution, 3
Journal of Peace Research, 3
journalism, ethics of, 4, 52; history
  of, 3-5
journalism education (see education
  in journalism)

Katz, Elihu, 123
Kelman, Herbert C., 77
Kennedy, John F., 36, 100
Kenya, 77
Khrushchev, Nikita, 36
Klapper, Joseph T., 8
Kolosov, Y.M., 93, 94
Korea, 61
Korean War, 21, 28, 86, 96
Kraft, Joseph, 18
Kruglak, Theodore E., 11
Kurtz, Harriet B., 45
Kurtz, Howard G., 45

Lamb, Curtis W., 32
Lambert, Richard D., 74
Larock, Victor, 114
Larsen, Otto N., 8
Lasswell, Harold D., 29
Latey, Maurice, 94
Lazarsfeld, Paul F., 10
Lenin, V. I., 97

values, shared, 46, 100-101
Van Dyke, Vernon, 31
Vietnam, 61, 74, 75
Vietnam war, 20, 38, 41, 49, 68,
   86, 96
Voice of America, 91, 103
"Voice of Peace," 126
Vreg, France, 50

Walker, Charles G., 4, 49
Wall Street Journal, 18
Walton, Richard E., 28, 42, 43, 47,
   57, 78, 92, 98, 103
war, 5, 22, 28
War/Peace Report, 3
Warsaw Pact, 45
Washburn, A. Michael, 63
Washington Post, 18
Watts, William, 23
Weidenfeld, Arthur, 28
Weiss, Walter, 8
Welch, Susan, 61

Werkheiser, Don, 36
White House Conference on Inter-
   national Cooperation, 112
White, Ralph K., 36, 37, 46, 91,
   101
Whiting, Alan S., 28, 96
Whyte, William H., Jr., 89
Wilhoit, G. C., Jr., 3
wire services, 16, 32, 33, 52-53,
   62, 72, 125
World Federalists, 49
World Health Organization, 108
World Law Fund, 63
World War I, 28
World War II, 28
Wright, Quincy, 5, 39

York, Herbert, 57
Yu, Frederick T. C., 17, 61
Yugoslavia, 94

Zajonc, Robert, 27

ADMINISTRATION OF THE FREEDOM OF
INFORMATION ACT: An Evaluation of
Government Information Programs Under
the Act, 1967-72

House Subcommittee on Foreign Operations and Government Information
foreword by Rep. William S. Moorhead

ASPEN NOTEBOOK ON GOVERNMENT AND
THE MEDIA Sponsored by the Aspen Program
on Communications and Society

edited by William L. Rivers
and Michael J. Nyhan

OPINION-MAKING ELITES IN YUGOSLAVIA

edited by Allen H. Barton, Bogdan
Denitch, and Charles Kadushin

THE ROLE OF COMMUNICATIONS IN THE
MIDDLE EAST CONFLICT: Ideological and
Religious Aspects

Yonah Alexander

SURVEILLANCE AND ESPIONAGE IN A FREE
SOCIETY: A Report by the Planning Group
on Intelligence and Security to the Policy
Council of the Democratic National Committee

edited by Richard H. Blum
foreword by Sen. Adlai Stevenson III

THE USES OF COMMUNICATION IN DECISION-
MAKING: A Comparative Study of Yugoslavia
and the U. S.

Alex S. Edelstein